S0-ATP-032

A GUIDE

PRAGUE CASTLE

History
Graphic and Photographic Illustrations
Fact and Fable
Rumour and Reflection
Information

freytag & berndt

a study by Jiří and Olga Melíškovi
with illustrations by Jan Kristofori
with photographs by Barbara Stenzel
graphic design by Studio ALBA, Prague
translated by Sarah Peters - Gráfová
published by © Freytag & Berndt, Prague, 1994

Cultural events at Prague Castle

Exhibitions:

In the Imperial Stables:

10th March - 8th may 1994

GEORG FLEGEL(1566 - 1638)
Organized in cooperation with the National Gallery in Prague and under the auspices of the Czech president Václav Havel and German President Richard von Weizsaker, this exhibition of still-life paintings and drawings by a significant Frankfurt artist is to be supplemented with a secondary exhibition of folk crafts from Flegel's time.

1th May - 30th October 1994

ALFONS MUCHA - posters, pastels and photography
An exhibition of the lesser-known work of this prominent early 20th century Czach artist, placing emphasis on Mucha's individuality of technique and expression.

And in the Maria Theresa Wing of the Old Royal Palace:

26th April - 26th June 1994

CITY CHANGES - Architecture of the City of London 1985-1995
An exhibition of plans and models submitted over the past decade by prominent world architects as suggestions for urban dvelopments in London. The exhibition, prepared by London's Architecture Foundation with the support of the british Council in London and Prague, is to be accompanied by an urban development symposium (taking place in the Ball-Game Lodge of the castle) organized by the Architecture Faculty of Charle's University in Prague.

Concerts:

13th May - 1st June 1994

Daily concerts in the Spanish Halll of Prague Castle as part of the 1994 Prague Sring Festival.

29th August - 4th September 1994

Cathedral Tribute - a musical project in celebration of the 650th anniversary of the laying of the foundation stone of St. Vitus' Cathedral.

"Vita brevis ars longa"
"Life is brief, Art constant..."

Hippocrates c. 400

...and so think carefully about how much time you would like to devote to looking at Prague Castle. Glance through the contents of this guide-book and decide on the pace which best suits you for wandering around the Castle grounds, although we recommend a *slow* pace. It's worth taking your time; a full and beautiful day lies ahead of you...

Guide Contents:

A. HOW TO REACH PRAGUE CASTLE...................................page 3

You will find your way there safely with the help of our maps. Even if your excellent sense of direction should fail you, there are plenty of people around who will be only too happy to point you in the right direction. There are various ways of approaching the Castle, but our suggestion is that you enter it from Hradčany Square. Once there, just follow section "E" of this guidebook.

**B. HOW TO ENJOY
THE VIEW OF PRAGUE FROM THE CASTLE**...................page 5

A panorama of facts and figures concerning Prague.

C. HOW TIME PASSED BY...page 12

The beginnings of Prague Castle; fact and legend;
a listing of Czech monarchs.

D. HOW NOT TO GET LOST IN PRAGUE CASTLE...............page 26

A general view of Prague Castle by Jan Kristofori. You can always use these illustrations to work out where you are.

E. YOUR ROUTE...page 25

A Guide to Prague Castle.
And we wish you fine weather for your tour...

F. TIME TO RELAX..page 91

A look at the Castle Gardens.

...and finally **INFORMATION**..page 106

St. Vitus' Cathedral (Chrám Sv. Víta)

B. HOW TO ENJOY THE VIEW

A panorama of facts and figures...

"Vidi!"
"I saw!"

... is what you'll soon be able to exclaim. And your memories will stay with you for years. It is best to enter the Castle from Hradčany square (Hradčanské náměstí), so that if you are approaching the Castle from another side we suggest that you first make your way to this Square, which is never far away once you are in the vicinity of the Castle. And that way you won't have to read our guidebook from back to front! So, here we are. Welcome!

This is the spot from which Prague Castle, since the end of the 9th century, has been entered by Kings and Dukes, Emperors and Emirs, Princes and Princesses, Popes and Presidents... and in just a moment it will be our turn.

From here we have one of the most beautiful views of Prague. From where? From there on the right, where all those people stand gazing into the distance and sighing with admiration. Just think how their neighbours are going to envy them those stunning holiday photographs! Squeeze your way in among the crowds and let yourself be transported by a magnificent vista of hanging gardens, a sea of houses, vaulted churches, the dusky gardens of Baroque palaces, ancient streets greeting one another in enchanting corners, and make sure that you turn around to admire the majestic defiance of the pinnacles of St. Vitus' Cathedral... this is Prague.

As you stand here now, as other travellers stood long before you, looking out into the distance and contemplating Prague. Some of their thoughts and impressions might just be of interest to you, so let's shift along a little and make room for them here... that's right... and let's admire the view together. Our first man went down in history with these observations:

"Prague is built from stone and lime and is the most prospering of towns as regards to trade. Russians and Slavs travel there with their wares, and Muslims and Jews and just as many Turks make their way there from the Turkish lands." **IBRAHIM IBN-HAKUB**, 965

"This town stretches up to the heavens in all her architectural splendour, with a core of magnificent streets upon which various businesses are being carried out. One place is given over to the sale of all manner of merchandise, another to the sale of meat on Saturdays, others are for the selling of fish, and others still do a trade in chickens. Here you'll see roosters that outstrip keen horses in price. They're sold here for thirty guilders, or often more." **UBERTO DE CEMBRIO**, 1399

Panoramic view of Prague from the approach to Hradčany Square (Hradčanské náměstí)

"The climate, the wholesomeness and the very cheer of this town; the nature of its society; and its clear view of an abundance of stars...are such that there are few towns in all of Germany to be compared with Prague." **TYCHO BRAHE**,1598

"In Prague there were during that period three times as many people as are usually there, and yet food was in abundance, so that even six men together were not able to eat their way through three ha'pennies' worth of bread. I bought myself a fatty, well fed goose on the market-place for just ninepence, and in one eating - house my brother and I ordered excellent roast meat with bread and beer, we ate until we could no more, and the whole cost us no more than fivepence! You can buy a fine turkey for two shillings, and I myself have never before seen such quantities of fresh fish. It is said that on just one market day two thousand carp are taken into Prague..." **J. TAYLOR**,1620

"The ladies there I found on the whole most pleasing, their figures luxuriant, blossoming." **J. W. FISCHER**,1801

"In general, Prague bears a strong resemblance to Paris. The houses are similarly white, the streets are equally muddy, and here, just as in Paris, horse- drawn cabs in dozens wait on the streets." **ARTUR SCHOPENHAUER**,1800

"The women of Prague are no less animated than the men of the town, and they have eyes which tell a tale more moving, more passionate than that which emanates from the blue eyes of the fair Saxon girls.

"Their stature too conforms more closely to the ideal. The Czech girl prides herself on the grace of her contours, for she is endowed with the most beautiful of feminine shapes, and she is moreover without the signs of plumpness found in those Elbe-dwelling Saxon girls... Their youthfulness, beauty and grace renders the girls of this town irresistible; and these enchantresses, it would appear, are not given to cruel treatment of their admirers..." **J. STRANG**, 1834

"Prague - as stately and as solemn as a widowed queen..."
COUNTESS L. THöRHEIM

"We see in the centre of Prague a vast, ancient, strikingly (and somewhat oddly) situated town which, after several centuries of perilous reversals of fortune, still remains; partly demolished, partially rebuilt, at times peopled, at times dispeopled, blossoming again and again into new life, and in recent times unfurling joyously into the far distance."
J. W. GOETHE, 1827

"Here they speak only of Figaro. They are all playing, singing, humming nothing but Figaro, which is of course a boundless honour for me... They are showering me with favours and gifts here, and Prague really is a beautiful and charming town, although I must admit to being already rather homesick again - " **W. A. MOZART**, 1787

"You beautiful town watched over by Hradčany, that stone king with a raised hand! Is there, anywhere, another town so rich as this, where Wallenstein's guns decay above the gates of palace gardens and a

View of Prague castle from the Smetana Embankent (Smetanovo nábřeží)

young nation is rising up to shape history with freedom...?"
HERMAN BANG, 1884

And some speculations from the more recent past:

"Prague lacks unity and is, I think, badly laid out. It is not possible to build much there."   **LE CORBUSIER**

"Prague is a golden argosy sailing majestically on the Vltava."
G. APOLLINAIRE

"There are cities pleasing and engaging, elegant and serene- and indeed there are many cities of beauty. But there are few cities of destiny, and Prague is one of them."   **V. V. ŠTĚCH**

Will Prague be for you too a "city of destiny" ...?

A STUDY IN FACTS AND FIGURES
Geographical location of Prague: 50°80' N, 14°32' E.
Average land height within Prague: 235 m a.s.l.
Highest point in Prague: 391 m a.s.l.

Wenceslas Square (Václavské náměstí): length 682,2 m, width at upper end 60,7 m, width at lower end 47 m.
Charles' Square (Karlovo náměstí): the largest square in Prague with a surface area of 80,500 m². Prague possesses 1,160 hectares of parkland and 2,520 hectares of woodland.
River Vltava: Within Prague's boundaries the Vltava possesses eight islands and nine tributary streams. Fifteen bridges span the river within Prague. The shortest of these is the Svatopluk Čech Bridge, and the widest is the Barrandov Bridge. The oldest is Charles' Bridge, construction of which began in 1357 on the site of the old Judith Bridge. The highest bridge in the city is that which crosses Nusle (in southern Prague) and has been in operation since 1973. Its length is 485 metres, its overall width 25,5 metres, and its highest point above ground level 43 metres.
At the beginning of the 19th century Bernardo Bolzano counted a total of 103 towers and spires in this city, so that Prague earned itself the adjective "hundred-spired". Today, however, the number of spires in Prague is estimated to be around 500. High-rise blocks are starting to creep in among them, although fortunately the construction boom in Prague isn't hitting too hard.

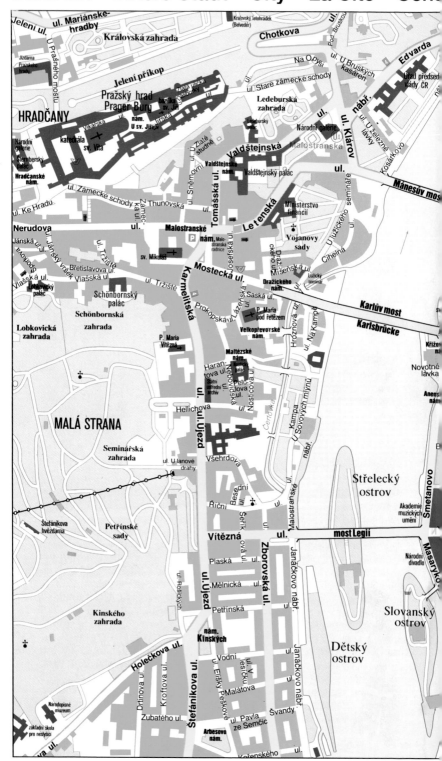

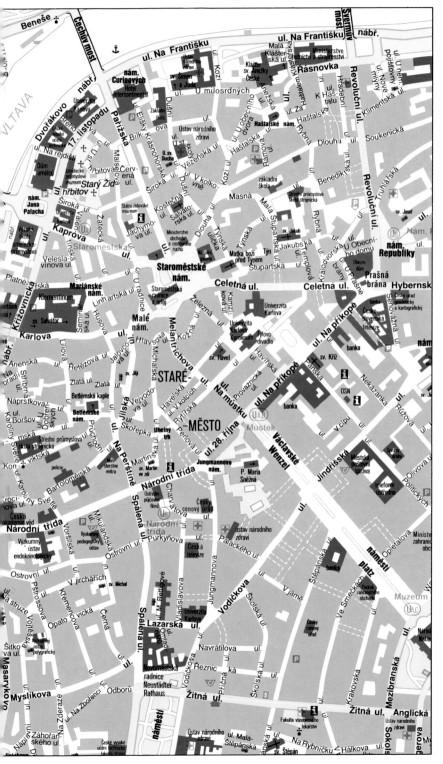

C. HOW TIME PASSED BY

The Beginnings of Prague Castle; the Romanesque and the Gothic

"Tempus silices et adamanta terit."

"Time smoothes the flint and the diamond."

Ovidius

Prague Castle is more than a thousand years old. Few places in the world have succeeded in preserving their historical atmosphere over such a long period of time whilst also having continued to function and to adapt throughout that same time. Thanks to a millenium of destinies, thanks to a thousand years of tradition (since the beginning of the 10th century Prague Castle has been the official residence of princes and the scene of royal coronations) and thanks to generations of craftsmen and builders and to wise rulers, a part of every individual era in history has been preserved here, and you will find that history with every step you take.

Let us take ourselves back to the historical beginnings of Prague Castle. Still today we can quote with relevance the unique and significant comments of Stocký (the first historian concerned with ancient Prague) on that obscure period:

"Pre-10th century sources are so fragmentary and indistinct that it is not possible to penetrate the gloom..."

And when it isn't possible to penetrate the mists of time, that's when legend comes into play...

According to the oldest Czech chronicle, that written by Cosmas (Dean of the Chapter of St. Vitus, died 1125), Prague Castle was founded by the legendary **Princess Libuše**. Her prophecy, in Cos-mas' reproduced form, became an actual historical source. Compulsory reading in Czech schools has long included the words of Jirásek, the classic author who placed the prophesying Princess Libuše, together with her husband and retinue, on a rocky slope high above the Vltava and wrote:

9th-century urn

And in an elated trance Libuše reached out her hand towards the bluish hillside beyond the river and, her eyes fixed on the forest there, uttered in a breath of prophecy:
"I see a vast city whose glory and fame shall reach the stars. In the forest there is a place not quite a league off, where the river Vltava winds its way. That place is encircled by the Brusnice stream to the north and by the rocky peak of Strahov woods to the south.

When you come there you will find, in the depths of the forest, a man hewing the threshold of a house, and the castle you erect upon that threshold shall bear the name "Prague". (Translator's note: Here the legend offers its Czech reader a theory as to the probable derivation of the name "Prague", the city's Czech name being "Praha" and "threshold" being rendered in Czech as "prah".)

And just as Princes and Dukes shall bow their heads before that threshold, so heads shall be bowed to our city. All praise and honour be unto that place, for it shall be of world renown." Here Libuše fell silent. She would have spoken further, but suddenly the ardent flame was extinguished in her, for the prophetic spirit had departed from her. And so they made their way beyond the river to the hill and entered the forest there and, finding there a man engaged in toil, as Libuše had foreseen and declared, they fell to building a castle in that very place. They built and they fortified, most particularly on the west side towards the Strahov woods, for the castle was here at this point most assailable. And they made too a deep moat, and a high bank with a timbered rampart on it, and here as well as above the gate they erected broad watchtowers. They drove wooden pins into the timbers and packed earth and straw in around them. They added mud walls to secure the timber against fire and flaming arrows. And so Castle Prague was well fortified, and reigned over the Czech Land.

A. Jirásek (Czech historical writer)

And now the verdict of our informed historians...

...the flow of the Vltava is responsible for having shaped Prague's distinctive land features. The city's history began with the arrival of the Slavs, following which the area of the river basin became a station on European trade routes. Frankish sources tell us that the title "Praganeo" (the name is given there by a certain "Bavarian geographer") was in use at the end of the 9th century to denote Prague's territory. Tradition has it that ancient Slavic cult sacrifices were once made on the piece of land where the Castle stands today.

The first well-known Přemyslid, **Prince Bořivoj (c. 870-894)**, was christened at the court of Svatopluk, the ruler of the Great Moravian Empire, and then founded **the Church of the Virgin Mary (Kostel Panny Marie)** on the elevation of land which is now Hradčany Hill. The foundations of the church lie exposed in the vicinity of the Prague Castle Picture Gallery. Bořivoj established the Castle as the seat of princely authority in the land. Whilst chronicles are lacking in first-hand information concerning the Castle's founding, the events laid out in various sources are at least concurrent with the information (gained through archaeological research) which we have concerning the Castle itself. Bořivoj's son **Vratislav I,** who was in permanent residence at the Castle, established within the Castle grounds a second church (905) dedicated to **St. George (sv. Jiří).** Vratislav ruled from 905-921.

After Vratislav's death the oldest of his

Helmet of St. Wenceslas
9th-10th century

two sons, Wenceslas (Václav), ascended to the throne. Until Wenceslas came of age his mother and grandmother ruled on his behalf, the controversy surrounding these two princesses reaching its culmination in the violent death of Ludmila, the grandmother. And this portended another death in the family. After 925 **Wenceslas** initiated the building of the **Rotunda of St.Vitus** in the very centre of the Castle territory, and soon after this a conspiracy arose among the magnates, leading to the murder of Wencelas whilst he was staying at the residence of his brother Boleslav. It was not easy to live as a prince in those times.

The bounds of the Castle territories towards the close of the 9th century and throughout the 10th century conformed more or less with those of today. The following information is the result of archaeological research and geological investigations.

The earliest fortifications comprised a line of deposited earth reinforced on the inner side with a timbered construction. The outer edge was lined with a wall of (dry applied) agillite, or clay slate. As regards to construction techniques, this walled settlement did not differ from others built in the central Czech lands during the 9th century. Rather more important is the fact that it was declared a dynastic residence. Now that the seat of the Přemyslid princes had been founded, there was nothing to stand in the way of the further development and economic prosperity of Prague. Under the prince's protection communities and marketplaces, established along those ancient traderoutes connecting the Czech lands with neighbouring territories, flourished greatly, and thus were laid the foundations of today's city.

Monarchs came and went, and the Castle grew. The new millenium began among fighting and bloodshed over who should rule the land. Discontent spread beyond the boundaries, and Emperor Henry III (Jindřich III) and his men besieged the Castle and set it on fire. The Castle was refortified by Prince **Břetislav I** (1034-d.1055), who added a huge stone wall, ramparts and a tower, and **Soběslav** (1125-d.1140) continued to augment the Castle in the Roman style. Fragments of his Romanesque fortification are preserved around the entire Castle periphery. A further siege and fire occurred in 1142, and building was again resumed under **Vladislav II**, who gained the crown in 1158. The last quarter of that century passed in heavy battling over the Czech throne. This period of internal strife did not end until the ceremonial coronation of King **Přemysl Otakar I** in 1198.

The Czech lands remained a kingdom after the year 1212. It seems appropriate to give here a chronological list of Czech monarchs, and

Crystal jug dating from middle of 14th century

so we will do just that. But not until the end of the chapter. Let us stop off again in the rule of **Přemysl Otakar I** and his son **Wenceslas I**, because it was under these men that the nation's military strength saw an unprecedented growth. The Czech King was the most powerful of the imperial princes. These two rulers again perfected the Castle's fortifications, something which was by now a great necessity; the settlements around the castle were swarming with the enemy. Dalimil, the author of another chronicle, bears witness to this...

Dalimil: The Tartar Invasion

In the year 1242 after the birth of our dear Lord Jesus Christ the "Kartassians" came. They were spies sent by the Tartars, and there were five hundred of them. They wore trousers with short gowns and extremely tall hats, and carried purses and long sticks. Whenever the desire came upon them to drink they would lie down on the river bank and drink there, and when they required bread they uttered the words "Kartas bob", and so they were known as the "Kartassians".They travelled as far as the Rhein and back. Oh, how rash and unwise was the tolerance with which the Czechs allowed these strangers to prowl throughout their territories and spy there. They should have ascertained the nature of these people, and not simply have allowed them to wander throughout the land. In the summer came the Tartars themselves, in three groups. They found their way around our country as if in their own land, for their spies led them. One of these groups had captured the great Russian town of Kiev, the second had overthrown the Hungarian King and the third had destroyed the whole of Poland, massacring Christians along its way.They had to stop just beyond Olomouc, for there they lost their Prince.Then they settled just outside Wroclaw, or Breslau. Prince Jindřich spoke out against them and met with a sordid end. The Tartars, bearing his head on a spear, proceeded to destroy the whole land.

The Czechs, meanwhile, in fear of the Tartars, took no rest from their work of building castles. The King had Prague enclosed with a wall and fenced in routes leading from the Castle down to the Vltava.

The Tartars destroyed Poland as far as Klodzko, or Glatz. Many men arrived from the German lands and moved off with the King in the direction of the Tartars. The Tartars retreated as soon as they heard of this, for their spies had warned them,"Fear none but the Czech King, who is not to be reckoned with."

Let us now pause to remember **Přemysl Otakar II** (1253-d.1278), who, co-ruling with his father Wenceslas I, initiated the rebuilding of the **Royal Palace** in 1252. A new domestic wing was added to the west side, followed by another wing on the east. The various buildings were connected by way of a covered arcade. Prague became an important centre within the Great Empire. But then Přemysl Otakar II, who was already aspiring to the imperial crown, fell in battle against Rudolf Hapsburg in Moravia 1278. Misfortunes rarely come singly, and after the fateful battle there came in 1280 an unprecedented gale which destroyed the Castle and other buildings. This natural catastrophe was then followed by Count Ota Brandenburg's grim news of the imprisonment of Wenceslas at Bezděz in northern Bohemia,and further disaster came in the form of fires, looting and starvation. The resilient Castle again made a recovery.The former glory of the royal residence was restored, and life returned; **Wenceslas II** (1278-d.1305), author of knightly ballads, ascended to the throne, and the Castle resounded with song. Period sources actually document the King's coronation...

The Zbraslav Chronicle (an extract-*The text refers to events of 1297.*)

An account of the costly preparations which were made for the King's coronation, and of the great number of guests present: In order that modesty should find no place in the coronation ceremony or in the grand and dignified celebration of the King's wealth, there was built, on a piece of beautiful and flat-lying land between Petřín Hill and the bank of theVltava, a Palace for the comfort of the King and his court, a palace of admirable dimensions and constructed with trimmed logs, the timbers being joined in such a way that the building should endure the ages. The Palace was raised a little above the ground just a little, so that entry and exit were by way of steps.There were tables and chairs and indeed everything which befits a festive banquet, as if the whole scene were the fabrication of some great artist. No detail had been overlooked. The gallery, the royal pavilion and the perimeter of the entire palace had been hung with priceless tapestries embellished variously with gold and silver and precious gemstones. Everything was carried out in perfect, spectacular fashion. Such a celebration as we then saw, a celebration which did itself credit by its very uniqueness, is surely to be commended by our descendants.

Oh, Prague, Prague! City of the great Kingdom, rejoice and be merry, because the song of joy is now yours. Day and night they stand on your very walls and shout their praises of your newly ordained one, King Wenceslas, and everywhere in your streets they sing aloud a song of exaltation and prosperity.

But may they conceive of it, or may their calculations bring them to conceive of it, just how great was the number of persons present and how vast the total sum expended, for, as I was informed by Lutold, esteemed parish priest (and in those days granger) from Ústí nad Orlicí, the Royal Court supplied fodder for the horses of all its guests and foreign visitors, who were in possession of no fewer than one hundred and ninety thousand beasts, and all this does not include the fodder which they distributed among the numerous residents of the locality and among those who belonged to the daily retinue, of whom there were not few. And on the new marketplace were fountains fed by underground pipes, and from those fountains the people drew wine, as if drawing water from a river. And neither can I merely pass in silence over the price which was being given during this coronation period for hen's eggs - eight hundred weighty talents! - and, should the reader be an able reckoner, I request him to inform me of the number of wine-drinkers present, who during that period would lay down twenty-four silver talents (Prague weight) merely for ice with which to cool their wine! May he write the figure here who knows it, for I myself hurry to move on to other matters and may tarry here no longer.

The period of Wenceslas II's rule is characterized by the growth of the Castle and the Czech lands. He implemented a currency reform and had the "Prague groschen" minted. It was the strongest currency in its day (c. 1300).

The era of Prague Castle's expansion and spreading fame began to draw to a close.The year following the death of Wenceslas II (1305) saw the murder of his son **Wenceslas III**, which brought about the extinction of the spear side of the first Czech dynasty.

Then came dispute over the vacated

Pewter jug

16

throne. In 1310 the assembly offered the throne, together with **Eliška,** the last remaining of the Přemyslids, to **John of Luxemburg**. He was a distinguished diplomat, politician and warrior, but neglected the Castle and his family. He let the Castle fall into disrepair and sent his son **Karel IV (Charles IV)** to the French court to be educated for battle.

Again, documentary evidence will perhaps acquaint us better with those times than will further storytelling.

This passage taken from the autobiography of Charles IV tells of his return to the Czech lands after eleven years' absence, and of his having to relearn the Czech language.

"...And then I came to the Czech lands, from which I had been absent for eleven years, to discover there that Eliška, my mother, had died some years before, and that my sister Guta, second-born, had been sent to France to marry John, the first son of the French King.

"And so I arrived in the Czech lands to find neither father nor mother, sister nor brother, nor any acquaintance whomsoever. I had forgotten our language utterly, and so had to study it again until I was able to understand and speak as any other Czech. And then by God's grace I learnt, besides Czech, also French, German and Latin, and the dialect of Lombardy, to the extent that I was equally at home in all of them with regard to reading, writing, speaking and understanding.

"At this time my father had set off for Luxembourg on account of a certain war in which he and his allies were engaged against the Brabantine Duke, father's allies being the Bishop of Liege, the Margrave of Julia, the Earl of Gerlen and many others. He handed over to me his authority in the Czech lands for the period of his absence. And I came upon a Kingdom so deserted that I was unable to find in it a single castle which had not already, and with its entire regalia, been pledged clean away, so that I had no other place to reside than in town houses, like an ordinary townsman. And Prague Castle itself was so decayed, had been since the days of King Otakar so badly damaged, destroyed, that it had made its way down to the very ground. And so I required the building of the large and beautiful palace, with all its refinements, which you see before you today.

"At this time I sent for my wife, for she was still in Luxemburg, and one year subsequent to her arrival she bore our first daughter, Margaret. And then my father bestowed upon me the Margraviate of Moravia, so that I enjoyed a new title. Then a company of honourable Czech men, seeing that I was of the old generation of Czech kings, kindly helped me to reobtain castles and royal posessions. I acquired a great many noble servants. The Kingdom prospered with every passing day, and I was well liked by my company of good men. Most of the noblemen had formerly been men of violence, unheeding of their fit and proper duty to fear their King, and they had divided the land among themselves. But now, in their fear, bad men eschewed evil, and so I ruled in the land, reforming with every passing day..."

Crown of the Czech kings, 1346

And it must be said that Karel was indeed an excellent ruler. The period of his reign was a remarkable era in the country's history. He stabilized the organization of the land and the power of its monarchy, and made Prague the seat of a king whose word held decisive sway in the events of the whole of central Europe.

After some time the old Palace was no longer able to accommodate Charles IV and his ambitions, so that the King embarked on a complete reconstruction of the building. His model, according to chroniclers, was the Royal Palace on the Seine. With the reinstitution of his Royal Palace, Charles laid the foundation stone (1344) of a new cathedral; St.Vitus' Cathedral was intended as a celebration of the city of Prague. The architect Matthias of Arras was given leave from France to build the presbytery after the style of the southern French cathedrals, and following Matthias' death, Charles authorized Petr Parléř, the son of a master-builder, to continue his work. The young Parléř immediately threw himself into the project, altering the ground plan, remodelling both the overall construction and its details. This whole new structure, against Matthias' design, was something quite new in Europe, a step in the direction of the exquisiteness and "visuality" of the Late Gothic. A complete gallery of busts of members of the royal family was installed into the triforium for future generations...
The Castle, its ground plan revived by a sensitive hand, now blossomed into the most magnificent residence in all of Europe.The culmination of the Gothic, or, we might say, a Gothic crown to set the seal upon Prague Castle's growth to date. Charles had built not simply a royal residence but an imperial centre.So, taking a deep bow in reverence to Charles IV, let us now return to the year 1212 for that promised chronological listing of Czech monarchs. We shall recall each monarch briefly, considering his significance in relation to Prague and to the Castle itself; although this is only a brief survey, as we want to move on quickly to our tour of the Castle.

Golden Cross of the Remains

View of St.Vitus' Cathedral from the east

Should you feel the desire to read a more thorough historical account than that which we have given here, then the following literature is to be recommended .
Zdeněk Wirth,I.Borkovský,V.aD.Mencl: Prague Castle in the Middle Ages,Prague 1946,
Rudolf Rouček: St.Vitus Cathedral (history and description of the Cathedral,Prague 1948)

THE CZECH MONARCHS

History and Legend have left us with the names of a great number of princes and princesses both real and imaginary. Legend gives us Libuše, who foretold the future glory of the city of Prague and its castle, and historical fact tells us of Přemysl Bořivoj, who first established princely authority there. However, let' s begin here with the first *crowned* ruler of the Czech lands, Přemysl Otakar I.

Přemysl Otakar I *ruled 1197-d. 1230*
The Czech lands were a kingdom from the year 1212. As we already know, Otakar made improvements to the security of the Castle's fortifications.

Wenceslas I (Václav I.) *born 1205, ruled 1230-d. 1253*
He founded Prague's Old Town (Staré město) during the years 1230-1232, and continued work on the Castle fortifications. A new style emerges - the Gothic.

Přemysl Otakar II
born 1233, ruled 1253-d. 1278
He founded the Lesser Town (Malá Strana) in 1257; otherwise see above (restructuring of the Royal Palace).

Přemysl Otakar (Gelhausen Manuscript)

Wenceslas II (Václav II.) *born 1271, ruled 1278-d. 1305*
He was given the crown of the Czech Kingdom in Prague Castle, and in 1300 (in Gniezna) Archbishop Peter invested him with the crown of the Polish Kingdom.

Wenceslas III (Václav III.)
born 1289, ruled 1305-d.1306
He was the last of the Přemyslids. In 1301 he was called to the Hungarian throne.

The last of the Přemyslids (Zbraslav Chronicle)

Henry of Corinth (Jindřich Korutanský) *first ruled in 1306*
He quarrelled with Rudolf Hapsburg over the Czech throne.

Rudolf Hapsburg *born 1281, ruled 1306-d. 1307*
He quarrelled with Henry of Corinth over the Czech throne.

Henry of Corinth (Jindřich Korutanský)
ruled for the second time 1307-1310, died 1335
He won in the dispute over the Castle and ruled for three years.

John of Luxembourg (Jan Lucemburský)
born 1296, ruled 1310-d. 1346
The district of Hradčany was founded in his reign. He was an incomparable knight and a warrior. However, the Czech crown succeeded in holding him down neither to the country nor to Prague Castle; he regarded his native Luxemburg as his true country, and felt more at home on the battlefields than in the Castle.

John of Luxemburg (Gelhausen Manuscript)

Charles IV (Karel IV.)
born 1316, ruled 1346-d. 1378
In 1348 he founded Prague's University and the New Town (Nové Město). He built on the Castle grounds and erected Charles' Bridge (Karlův most) and a whole array of other buildings. We have already taken a deep bow to him here.

Charles IV-
detail from a votive painting by Jan Očko

Wenceslas IV (Václav IV.) *born 1361, ruled 1378-d. 1419*
He continued work on St. Vitus' Cathedral and built a new wing onto the Castle-the King's Suites. He inclined towards the refined architectural style.

Sigismund (Zikmund) *born 1368, ruled 1419-d. 1437*
He was at once both Hungarian King and Holy Roman Emperor. He ordered the possession of precious metals and gemstones from St. Vitus' Cathedral, in order to pay his soldiers. The Czech Kings of this period resided in the Kings' Court, which was located on and around the site of the present-day Obecní dům (Municipal House) in Prague.

Albrecht Hapsburg
born 1397, ruled 1438-d. 1439
The Castle degenerates in a succession of wars.

Ladislav Pohrobek *born 1440, ruled until death in 1457*
Wars and quarrels over occupation of the throne continue, and the Castle degenerates further.

George of Poděbrady (Jiří Poděbradský)
born 1420, ruled 1458-d. 1471
More peaceful times, at last. Following so many battles, the Castle remained during his reign no more than a mere symbol of royal residence.

Vladislav II of Jagiello
(Vladislav II. Jagelonský)
born 1456,ruled 1471-d. 1516
He built onto the Castle the adjoining Vladislav Hall, and strengthened the Castle fortifications. He also built a new wall, with three towers which were given the names White Tower (Bílá věž), Daliborka and Mihulka. The Vladislav Hall was built by Benedict Ried, and Vladislav's various modifications of the Castle stand as an

Motiv from the Matthias Gate

excellent monument to the Czech Gothic. Elements of the Renaissance also appear for the first time during this period. The Vladislav Hall is unique from a constructional point of view, unparallelled particularly as regards its foundations and overall dimensions. Benedict Ried was knighted.

Louis (Ludvík) *born 1506, ruled 1516-d. 1526*
He is known for his having admired that which his father had had built, rather than for having carried out a great amount of work himself.

Ferdinand I Hapsburg
(Ferdinand I. Habsburský)
born 1503, ruled 1526-d. 1564
Ferdinand agreed to rule from Prague, although he was frequently called away by administrative duties in other countries and by wars with the Turks. His wife Anna remained in Prague. Following her death in 1547 their son Ferdinand Tyrol became vice-regent. The medieval Castle now no longer met the needs of the royal fam-

Ferdinand I and his wife Anna-
Royal Summer Palace

ily, so that costly reconstructions were carried out. An extensive complex of gardens emerged, and the Castle regained its former beauty... until June 1541, when a disastrous fire struck the Castle, the heat from the flames being so great as to melt the Cathedral bells. It took years to clear the damage. Here we should mention Boniface Wohlmut, who succeeded in covering the traces of the fire, primarily in his restoration of the Hall of the Diet.

Maximilian II (Maxmilián II.) *born 1527, ruled 1564-1576*
He is responsible for having ornamented the Castle, rather than for

having built upon it. The bronze fountain in the King's garden was completed and work was begun on a new Castle wing, and Oldřich Arostalis erected a chapel over the tomb of St. Adalbert (sv. Vojtěch).

Medal depicting Rudolf II.

Rudolf II *born 1552, ruled 1576-1611, died 1612*
He supplemented the Castle with a number of large halls which he filled with his collections. Prague became a centre of artistic activity. Scientists, artists and charlatans from all over the world came to the Castle. Among the well-known scientists who visited were the celebrated astronomers Tycho Brahe and Johannes Kepler, both of whom achieved significant portions of their lives' work here.

Matthias (Matyáš)
born 1557, ruled 1611-d.1619
He made partial alterations to the Castle and built the New Matthias Gate (Nová Matyášova brána).

Motif from the Matthias Gate (Matyášova brána)

Frederick Palatine (Friedrich Falcký)
born 1596, ruled 1619-1620, died 1632
Vienna became the centre of the land. The brief reign of Frederick Palatine (the "Wintry King") saw the fall of the Cathedral into the hands of the iconoclasts.

Ferdinand II Hapsburg (Ferdinand II. Habsburský)
born 1578, ruled 1619 (1620)-d.1637
The restored Castle became the family residence of the Hapsburgs.

Ferdinand III *born 1608, ruled 1637-d.1657*
A time of intensive building activity at the Castle. The Empress's rooms were built to the east of the Rudolf Palace; a new approach to the Castle (from the present-day Neruda Street) was constructed; and the gardens were redesigned after the Baroque style.

Ferdinand IV *born 1633, crowned 1646, died 1654*

Leopold I *born 1640, ruled 1657-d.1705*
His reign saw the culmination of the Early Baroque in Prague Castle. A small operatic stage was built in the Royal Gardens and a fountain in

the Second Courtyard. The foundation stone of the Baroque completion of St. Vitus' Cathedral was laid in 1673.

Josef I *born 1678, ruled 1705 - d.1711*

Charles VI (Karel VI) *born 1685, ruled 1711-d.1740*
In 1723 Charles built a theatrical stage for the performance of Fux's
grandiose opera "Constanza e Fortezza", in honour of his wife (Eliza-
beth Christina) and of the coronation of the Royal couple.

Maria Theresa (Marie Terezie) *born 1717, ruled 1740-d.1780*
She altered Prague Castle into its present-day form under the super-
vision of Viennese court architect Nicolo Pacassi. The Castle, being
located out of the way of events, now became deserted.

Josef II Hapsburg-Lotringian (Josef II. Habsbursko-lotrinský)
born 1741, ruled 1780-d.1790
In 1784 he joined the four towns of Prague into one-divesting Prague,
of its status as royal residence. The Castle's importance futher dwin-
dled. The grounds were given over to the army and the royal collections were sold off.

Leopold II *born 1747, ruled 1790-d.1792*
The Castle was restored to life for Leopold's coronation, but then fell
yet again into a state of provincial destitution.

Tribute to Ferdinand V on the Third Courtyard of Prague Castle (1836)

Franz I (František I.) *born 1768, ruled 1792-d.1835*

Ferdinand V *born 1793, ruled 1835-1848, died 1875*
His coronation in Prague Castle was a formal display of beauty things.
The Castle continued to serve predominantly as a mere stop-over residence until the middle of the 19th century, when the Castle became
the home of Ferdinand himself (now former Emperor and Czech King,
and known as "Ferdinand the Benign"). He resided there until the end

of his life, with his wife Marie Anna of Sardenia.

Franz Josef I (František Josef I.) *born 1830, ruled 1848-d.1916*
He carried out alterations to the Spanish Hall and the Rudolf Gallery, the latter being intended as the venue for the (unrealized) coronation of the Emperor.

Charles (Karel) *born 1887, ruled 1916-1918, died 1922*
On the 28th of October 1918 the rule of the Hapsburg-Lotringen line came to an end and the Czech Kingdom was extinguished by the declaration of the existence of a new and independent state and so our list continues with the presidents of this new state.

Tomáš Garrique MASARYK *1918-1935*
Masaryk, philosopher and Charles' University professor, entered the Castle on 21st December 1918 as the first Czechoslovak President. Josip Plečnik, Castle Architect from 1920, carried out modifications of the First and Third Courtyards, the President's quarters and library, and the Hall of Columns, as well as of the Paradise Garden, Garden on the Bastion, and the steps into the garden on the Ramparts.

Dr. Edvard BENEŠ *1935-1938; 1945-1948*
Pavel Janák, Castle Architect from 1936, carried out alterations suggested by Beneš. The pre-war period saw the renovation of the Maria Theresa Wing, the reconstruction of the Royal Summer Palace garden and the addition of a Marble Hall on the first floor of the south wing, by the White Tower.

Klement GOTTWALD *1948-1953*
During this period Janák made alterations to the Riding School and designed the President's Lodge (built 1949) in the Royal Garden.

Antonín ZÁPOTOCKÝ *1953-1957*
Janák completed alterations to the Charles and Wenceslas Halls of the Old Royal Palace and restored the Royal Summer Palace. In 1954 the President's Office took over the care of St. Vitus' Cathedral. Janák's successor was Jaroslav Frágner, who from 1959 worked on reconstructing the Central Wing of the Castle.

Antonín NOVOTNÝ *1957-1968*
The Burgoaster's House was converted into the House of Czechoslovak Children, the Vikárka modernized, the Castle Picture Gallery built and the St. Wenceslas Chapel restored.

Ludvík SVOBODA *1968-1975*
He suggested that St. George's Church be given over for the use of the National Gallery and a permanent Czech history exhibition be installed in the Lobkovic Palace.

Dr. Gustav HUSÁK *1975-1989*
This period saw a number of unfortunate changes such as removal of Masaryk's library and alterations to the entrance to the Spanish Hall and the Rudolf Gallery.

Václav HAVEL *1989-*
The Castle was brought to life again, and parts of it made newly accessible. Alterations have been made to the President's Lodge (Royal Garden). The Great Ball-Game Lodge, Rudolf's Stables and the Foundry Courtyard have been restored,and the Castle Picture Gallery is to be opened.

Since 1st January 1993 Prague Castle has towered above the capital city of a new and independent Czech Republic.

E. YOUR ROUTE

A Guide to Prague Castle

"per pedes apostoloru..."
On our feet, as did the Apostles go...

(And here you may proceed as you wish. Should you be in a hurry, then forget relaxed contemplation and our red-marked route until your next visit. But we suggest rather that you take your time here. The day is a favourable one, and you are standing now on one of the most beautiful of all squares.)

Whilst there is a number of possible approaches to the Castle, we have chosen to come by way of Hradčany Square. Unfortunately, not all guests who passed through here were invited ones and the Castle was always most vulnerable on this side, so that systems of mounds and ditches, walls and ramparts were constructed against prospective invaders.

View of St. Vitus' Cathedral

D. HOW NOT TO GET LOST IN PRAGUE CASTLE

Illustrations by Jan Kristofori

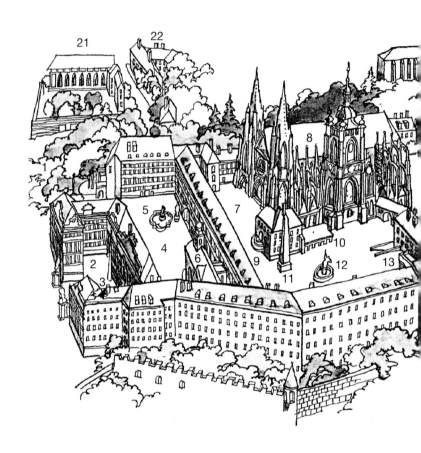

1. Garden on the Bastion
2. First Courtyard
3. Matthias Gate
4. Second Courtyard
5. Kohl Fountain
6. Chapel of the Holy Rood
7. Third Courtyard
8. St. Vitus' Cathedral
9. The Old Provost' s Residence
10. Archeological excavations
11. The Monolith
12. Statue of St. George

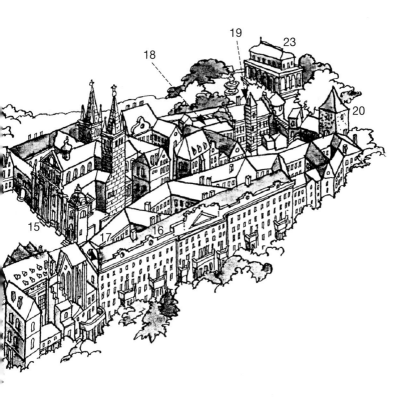

13. The Old Royal Palace
14. George Square
15. The Basilica of St. George
16. The Institute of gentlewomen
17. George Street
18. Golden Lane
19. The Old Burgomaster's House
20. The Black Tower
21. The Riding School
22. Lion Court
23. The Royal Summer Palace

Panoramic view of Prague's Hradčany and Lesser Town (Malá strana)

Prague Castle and the view across the city from Hradčany Square

Midday Changing of the Guard on the First Courtyard

Entrance to the First Courtyard
You are standing before the entrance gates between Hradčany Square and the First Courtyard. On the pillars which frame these gates you can see two group statues of wrestling giants, and other columns are decorated with vases, eagles, lions, cherubs and ancient heraldic emblems. All these decorations (created in 1769-1771 by I.F. Platzer) may still be admired by us today only on account of the fact that the originals, made of soft sandstone, were replaced by sturdier reproductions in 1902.

The Castle Guard
Beneath the menacing giants stand the no less admired and photographed young men of the Castle Guard. It becomes them here, and no wonder: they wear uniforms designed (in 1989) by Theodor Pištěk, the artist who won an Oscar for his designs for the film Amadeus (1984), a prize for his work on the film Valmont (1990), as well as other prestigious awards. But let us get back into history. Having walked through the giant-topped gates past the photogenic guards, you are now standing in the newest part of the whole Castle complex.

The First Courtyard
The Courtyard is surrounded on three sides by buildings (dating from 1763-1771) in the style of the Viennese Rococo and influenced by French Classicism. Reconstruction was carried out according to

designs by the Viennese architect N. Pacassi, whose name we shall be seeing a considerable amount of here. The clearly defined and precise-even rigid-nature of his work is softened and humanized to a certain extent here by the presence of classical antiquity in the form of ancient gods and the giants at the entrance gates. These buildings are given over to state functions.

Centuries ago, the house of the Keeper of the Imperial Collections stood here on the left. Various craftsmen lived here too, including the court locksmith. Even an armoury once stood in the vicinity.

The right-hand wing of the building now houses special apartments for state visits. In front of the west wing two ceremonial flagpoles tower 25 metres high.

The Matthias Gate (Matyášova brána)

Behind these flagpoles there arches a remarkable stone gate from the early Baroque: the Matthias Gate, as it is named, in honour of its institutor, the Emperor Matthias (Matyáš). We know for certain that the gate was built in 1614. What we are not so sure of, however, is who actually built it. The designer is imagined to be one of two architects, G. M. Philippi or V. Scamozzi. The Gate once stood independently, overlooking the moat of the Castle, but Pacassi incorporated it into the main building whilst carrying out reconstruction work on this Courtyard. The top of the Gate bears an inscription in honour of Emperor Matthias, with an enumeration of his titles, and on the gate can be seen the emblems of those countries under his supremacy, from left to right: Upper Lusatia, Luxemburg, Lower Austria, Bohemia, the Holy Empire, the Hungarian Lands, Silesia, Moravia and Lower Lusatia.

If you step through the Matthias Gate into the passageway you will see that a staircase leads upwards on either side. The grandiose ceremonial staircase on the right dates from the time of Maria Theresa and leads up to the State Rooms. One of these is the Throne Room, in

The Matthias Gate

which foreign diplomats are received by the President, and other rooms of note here include the Hapsburg Salon (which takes its name from the Hapsburg family gallery), the Hall of Mirrors, the Music Room and the Brožík Hall (named after the Czech painter whose paintings adorn its walls).This same staircase also carries state visitors up to their special quarters. This section of the Castle is made accessible to the public only very rarely and in the most exceptional circumstances.

Brožík hall

The Habsburg Salon

The Second Courtyard

The Matthias Gate has brought you through the West Wing of the Castle into the Second Courtyard, which is not only wider and longer than the First, but also older. It evolved gradually from the beginning of the 16th century, by which time the Hapsburgs were already on the throne. Originally it was not enclosed on all sides by buildings, as the old fortification (wall and towers) still ran along its front end. The remains of the White Tower (Bílá věž) are preserved in the wall in the corner to the right. The White Tower was an impressive Romanesque structure and by the beginning of the 12th century was functioning as state prison. It is said that Rudolf II later ordered his master-builder to redesign the Tower so that he, Rudolf, could observe the stars in comfort from its ramparts and cast horoscopes. His quarters were immediately adjacent to the Tower and he must have had a beautiful view over the city from them. The section of building which forms the right-hand portion of the Second Courtyard enclosure passed through a complex and multistage evolution. It attained its present appearance during the reign of Maria Theresa (1753-1775).

The Chapel of the Holy Rood (Kaple sv. Kříže)

The Chapel of the Holy Rood, which juts out into the Courtyard, was built between 1756 and 1764 by A. Lugaro on the site of the former Building Commission offices. One hundred or so years later it underwent its first reconstruction. Statues of St. Peter and Paul were added. The Chapel comprises a nave and a semicircular sacristy. Above the gallery are five oratories with grilles, and paintings on the walls and vault depict scenes from the Old and New Testaments.The Chapel attained its present-day appearance in the second half of the 19th century. The original altar remains.

The Rudolf Gallery (Rudolfova galerie)

The Wing across the Courtyard (to the north) comprises the Spanish Hall and the Rudolf Gallery.
We already know that Rudolf II was a great lover not only of all the sciences, but also of art. He obtained treasures from all over the world

The Rudolph Gallery

and lodged them in his Imperial Collections, and when his Palace became quite overfull with art jewellery and various other curiosities he opted for a radical solution: he had this Gallery built (in 1597-98) by G.Gargiolli, above the old stables facing the Palace.

Rudolf's original collections were really unique in Europe, although little remains of them now; some items were taken off to Vienna after the Thirty Years' War, whilst others were stolen by the Swedes in 1648. However, it is still worth taking a look, as the collections have been gradually supplemented and today they house some excellent works of art; Titian, Rubens, Tintoretto, Feti, van Haarlem and many others are represented here, and you will see a remarkable bronze sculpture collection.

The Spanish Hall (Španělský sál)

The building of the Spanish Hall was initiated by Gargiolli and completed by Philippi. Fundamental reworking was then undertaken by I. Dientzenhofer and A. Lugaro, who removed pillars, added a new roof and laid parquet flooring, only to meet with extremely bad luck; in 1757 Prussian army fire destroyed their work.

In 1836 the original frescoes were covered over when the Hall was decorated with mirrors for the occasion of the coronation of Ferdinand V. The most recent modifications to the Hall were made in 1865-68 in preparation for the coronation (which never actually took place) of Franz Josef I.

[Note: In this Wing there is also a passageway which will take you, should you not be in too much of a hurry, on a brief excursion out of the Castle grounds by way of the Riding School (Jízdárna) and Lion's Yard (Lví dvůr), in the direction of the Powder Bridge (Prašný most).]

The Kohl Fountain (Kohlova kašna)

In the centre of the Courtyard stands a beautiful Baroque fountain dat-

The Spanish Hall

The Well (Second Courtyard)

ing from 1686, the work of Francesco de Torre, although it is named "Kohl" after the sculptor who added the relief work.

The Well (Studna)

Nearby you can see an extremely old well surrounded and enclosed by a flattering wrought grille which dates from the beginning of the 17th century and is somewhat reminiscent of a large birdcage. Servants, soldiers and travellers once stood here waiting to draw water, chatting about current events and exchanging jokes and news. Here are some of their stories...

William II (Vilém II), whilst inspecting his troops, always liked to address his soldiers with a number of questions, which he always put to the men in precisely the same order: "How long have you been serving? How old are you? Are your parents still alive?" So that the soldiers always had their answers prepared in advance and, of course,

in the correct order. Once, during inspection, William chose to reverse the order of his questions, addressing his first soldier:

"How old are you?"

"Four years."

"How long have you been serving?"

"Twenty-five years."

The Emperor paused, considered, and then exclaimed,

"Lord God! Are you stupid or am I?"

And of course the reply came,

"Both, Your Majesty."

The Prussian King Friedrich II possessed a sense of humour. On one occasion a royal soldier was found out to have money on his person, money which was known to have been donated by devout members of the Silesian Church in honour of the Virgin Mary. The soldier denied having stolen the money, insisting that in his great need he had prayed to the Virgin Mary so imploringly that She herself had bestowed the money on him. In spite of these claims he was given over to the military courts and his case submitted to the King himself. The King first called upon the Catholic priests for their expert opinion, inquiring of them as to whether the teachings of their church might accommodate the possibility of such a miracle. When the priests replied in the affirmative the King drafted his verdict as follows: "The Accused is pardoned on the basis not only of his own denial of the theft but also of expert theological advice, which allows that the possibility of the occurrence of such a miracle is not to be ruled out utterly. However, future repetition of the incident shall result in the most severe punishment, so that it is from this moment strictly forbidden for him to accept gifts of money from the Virgin Mary or from any other Saint whomsoever. Fridericus rex."

And finally, an anecdote concerning the simpler folk of Prague: A poor monk was leading an offender from the Black Tower to the execution ground in rainy weather. On their way the condemned man lamented, reproaching God bitterly for the fact that he was having to undertake this last mournful journey in such cheerless weather. The monk, wishing to console him a little, said. "But why do you lament so, my son? You have to make only the one journey. I am to walk all the way back again in this wretched weather !"

The **Central Area** of the Castle, separating the West and East Wings, underwent a slow and gradual evolution. There once stood here a Romanesque fortification incorporating the White Tower and the Bishop's Tower. Houses appeared to the east of the White Tower by the Middle Ages.The moat was filled in and, later, the stone wall taken down, although happily not in its entirety. A part of it still remains preserved today, as does a fragment of the walkway which Rudolf II had built in order that he should not get his feet muddy whenever he wanted to make his way across the Courtyard to be among his treasures in the Castle Picture Gallery.

The Central Wing

In the middle of the 17th century Ferdinand III had a new Palace built here by the architect Mathey. In 1760-1775 the work of architect A. Haffenecker followed designs by Pacassi to give the whole Courtyard its present- day appearance, the two Towers and parts of the old wall being incorporated into the new design. The White Tower (Bílá věž), as we have already mentioned, is still (partially) preserved in the right-hand corner of the Courtyard, and the Bishop's Tower (Biskupská věž) stood to the left (that is, to the north) of the White Tower. The remains of the Romanesque fortification itself are still to be seen in the passageway through which you will soon pass into the Third Courtyard.

St. Vitus' Cathedral and the Third Courtyard
You are now entering into the oldest part of the Castle precinct. This is the very place from which Czech princes were ruling over the land as early as a thousand or more years ago. During the course of time

Western facade of St. Vitus' Cathedral

these older parts of the Castle have of course undergone physical change, although their function remains unaltered. This has always been a place not only of ceremony and grandeur, but also of great mystery. And we can still feel that mystery as we stand here today.

The Cathedral

As soon as we step into the Courtyard we cannot fail to be astounded by the magnificence of the huge facade of St.Vitus' Cathedral. At last we can to take a closer look at the Cathedral which, with its elegant spires, sets off the harmonious shapes of the castle. St. Vitus' is, indeed, the Crown of Prague Castle and its evolution is long and complex...

A sanctuary stood on this site during the reign of Prince Wenceslas in the 10th century, and later a Romanesque Basilica (completed in 1096). The foundation stone of the Gothic Cathedral was laid in 1344 when the Pope elevated Prague's status to that of Archbishopric. Charles IV chose as his master-builder the Frenchman Matthias of Arras (Matyáš z Arrasu), who brought plans with him from his native France.

Following Matthias' death, work was continued by Petr Parléř of Gmünd, and then by his sons after him. Building progressed slowly, and then ceased altogether for several decades. There were periods of activity and revolution (the period of the Hussite Wars). And then in 1541 a fire which destroyed not only the Cathedral, but the entire Castle. In 1620 the Calvinists plundered the area, and in the following century the Prussians fired their guns at it. Finally, as if Nature herself were against the completion process, 1760 saw the tearing down, by lightning, of the Cathedral's then only spire.The Castle attained its present-day form between 1873 and 1929.

This Gothic Cathedral is the largest church in Prague and is of exceptional significance in terms of the nation's history. This is the burial place of the Czech Kings, the home of the Crown Jewels and both St. Wenceslas and St. John of Nepomuk lie buried here.

The Cathedral has three spires. The oldest, that which was once struck by lightning, stands to the east and has a height of 965 metres. The two slim spires at the head of the Cathedral each measure 82 metres and are much more recent.

Should you have little time to spare, then please feel free to skip over the following description of the interior of the Cathedral and proceed straight to the Third Courtyard...

The Cathedral entrance comprises of three bronze doors depicting sce-nes from the lives of the Saints: Saint Wenceslas (Václav) on the left, and St. Adalbert (Vojtěch) on the right. The central door is decorated with scenes from the history of the construction of the Cathedral.

You will be astonished the moment you step inside! A vast space stretches before you, cool and monumental, a nave with an endlessly long vault supported by twenty- eight tall pillars.

Interior of St.Vitus' Cathedral

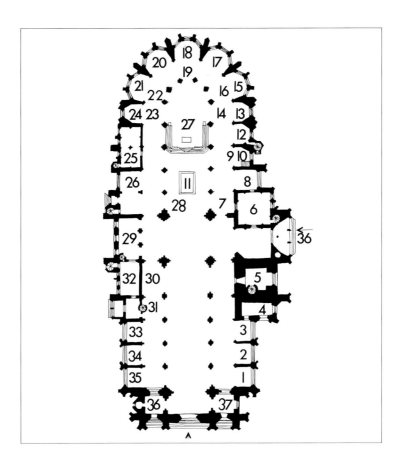

St. Vitus' Cathedral

1   Chapel of St. Ludmila
2   Chapel of the Tomb of God
3   Thun Chapel
4   Chapter library
5   Hasenburg Chapel (southern tower)
6   Chapel of St. Wenceslas
7   Epitah of Count Leopold Šlik
8   The Martinitz Chapel
9   Chapel of the Holy Rood
10 Entrance to the Crypt of
    the Czech Kings
11 The Royal Tomb
12 The Royal Oratory
13 Wallestein Chapel
14 Early Baroque woodcuts
15 Chapel of St. John of Nepomuk
16 Tomb of St. John of Nepomuk
17 Saxon Chapel of the Holy Remains
18 Chapel of Our Lady
19 Altar of St. Vitus
20 Chapel of St. John the Baptist

21 The Arcibishops' Chapel
22 Memorial to Cardinal Schwarzenberg
23 Early Baroque woodcuts
24 Chapel of St. Anne
25 The Old Sacristy
26 Chapel of St. Sigismund
27 Choir and main altar
28 Pulpit
29 The Choir Chapel
30 Bílek's altar with Christ on the Cross
31 Staircase to the Cathedral Treasury
32 The New Sacristy
33 The New Archbishops' Chapel
34 The Schwarzenberg Chapel
35 Chapel of St. Anne of Bohemia
36 The Golden Portal
37 Chamber below south-west tower
38 Chamber below north-west tower

Bust of Petr Parléř in the triforium gallery of St. Vitus' Cathedral

The Dimensions of the Cathedral
The Cathedral is 124 metres in length. Its maximum width is 60 met-res, and the vault of its nave is 33 metres high. Construction of the Cathedral was carried out in two main periods in history, so that we may divide the entire structure into two `sections'. The choir, chapels, and main spire belong to the earlier period (the 14th and15th cen-turies), the foundation stone of the Gothic Cathedral having been laid on the 21st November 1344. The triple nave (main nave and two aisles), the transverse nave and the two western spires appeared in the latter half of the 19th century and at the beginning of the 20th, the builders of this period continuing within the old scheme. Only the main entrance and facade perhaps do not follow exactly the intentions of Matthias of Arras and Petr Parléř.

The Gallery
The edges of the vault are supported by impressive pillars which cre-ate arcades. The triforium above contains a gallery housing twenty-one busts of various royal family members, archbishops and all those of significance in the evolution of the Cathedral, including of course Matthias of Arras and Petr Parléř. The busts date from 1374 - 1385.
The first side chapel to the right of the main entrance is that of **St. Ludmila** (1849), followed by the **Chapel of the Tomb of God** and then the **Thun Chapel**, in the corner of which there are doors leading off to the Chapter Library. The **Hasenburg Chapel** forms the base of the Main Tower of the Cathedral.

The Main Tower
On the first floor is "Sigismund" - the largest bell in Bohemia. It weighs seventeen tons and is two metres high and two and a half metres in diameter. The bell was cast in 1549.

The transverse nave of St. Vitus' Cathedral (view from the south)

Chapel of St. Wenceslas (Kaple sv. Václava)

The first Chapel beyond the transverse nave is old and beautiful and one of the most famous here, as it is that of St. Wenceslas, patron saint of the Czech lands. It is located where once stood the apse of the Romanesque Rotunda in which Wenceslas was originally buried, and it represents the culmination of the Czech Gothic. Its decorative work stands as evidence of the skill of the old masters.

The Chapel of St. Wenceslas was built in 1362-67 by Petr Parléř. Its lower part is adorned with semiprecious stones and paintings from 1372 depicting the sufferings of Christ. There is also a portrait of Charles IV with his fourth wife, and above a ledge are 16th-century depictions of scenes from the life of St. Wenceslas. Wenceslas's poly-chrome statue, which stands on the ledge, was produced by Parléř in his foundry in 1373. The altar table below the statue dates from the 14th century. Wenceslas lies buried almost in the very centre of the Chapel. His tombstone, of the 14th century, was restored at the begin-ning of the 20th century by K. Hilbert.

In the corner of the Chapel is a staircase leading to the Coronation Chamber (home of the Crown Jewels). The iron doors here are secured with seven locks, the keys to which are kept by seven repre-sentatives of church and state.

The Chapel of the Holy Rood (Kaple sv. Kříže)

and the Archaeological Excavations Beyond the Chapel of St. Wenceslas you will find the **Chapel of St. Andrew**, followed by the Chapel of the Holy Rood. Both are the work of Petr Parléř, whilst Matthias of Arras also participated in the construction of the latter. From this Chapel you can follow steps leading down and back into the10th and 11th centuries, for here are preserved the remains of the Romanesque Basilica with a fragment of its altar. A line of pillars once supported its vaulting.

The Chapel of St. Wenceslas, St. Vitus' Cathedrall

49

Detail from the silver tomb of St. John of Nepomuk

The Crypt of the Czech Kings, St. Vitus' Cathedral

The Crypt of the Czech Kings (Královská krypta)

The Crypt was modified in the earlier part of this century (1928-35), and the sarcophagi are likewise new. Charles IV, who died in 1378, lies buried in the centre of the Crypt, and his children and four wives are buried here too. Rudolf II's coffin is of tin. Other Kings buried here include George of Poděbrady (Jiří z Poděbrad) and Ladislav Pohrobek. The **Royal Tomb** is located directly above this spot in the overground part of the Cathedral, just in front of the high altar.

Adjacent to the Chapel of the Holy Rood is the **Royal Oratory** of 1493, and beyond it the **Wallenstein Chapel**, containing the tombs of the Wallenstein family and of Matthias of Arras and Petr Parléř.

The Chapel of St. John of Nepomuk
(Kaple sv. Jana Nepomuckého)

The next chapel in the line is that of St. John of Nepomuk, whose (Baroque) silver tomb is located in the triforium. The cover of this 1736 tomb bears the figure of a saint with angels. A marble balustrade dating from 1746 incorporates a ledge upon which stand allegorical statues, and angels support a canopy above the coffin.

The Chapel of St. Mary (Kaple sv. Marie)

After the **Chapel of the Holy Remains** (also Saxon), and at the very head of the main nave, is the Chapel of St. Mary, also known as the

St. Vitus' Cathedral, view of the Choir from the Royal Tomb

Woodcut (by Bechteler) and Memorial to Cardinal Schwarzenberg (by Myslbek)

Imperial Chapel, and founded by Charles IV himself. It is probable that the construction of the Gothic Cathedral was begun in this very place in 1344. The Chapel was consecrated in 1368. The Přemyslids lie buried in the Gothic side-tombs here, and facing this Chapel the triforium holds the Altar and Holy Remains of St. Vitus.

If we continue along the north side of the Cathedral we come first to the Chapel of St. John the Baptist (**Kaple sv. Jana Křtitele**), with its tombs of Czech princes, and then to the **Archbishops' Chapel (Kaple arcibiskupská)**, below which a succession of Prague's archbishops lies buried. Not far from this chapel is the impressive memorial to Cardinal Bedřich Schwarzenberg, created by J.V. Myslbek in 1892-95. The adjacent **Chapel of St. Anne (Kaple sv. Anny)** stands above the Nostitz family crypt and contains an altar into which is set a silver relic panel. This early Gothic panel, dating from the latter half of the 13th century, was stolen from the Church of St. Martin in Trier during the French Revolution and donated to the Cathedral by Count Nostitz in 1846.

The Old Sacristy (Stará sakristie)
And now we follow on immediately to the Old Sacristy, formerly the Chapel of St. Michael, on the walls of which you can see portraits of Prague's archbishops. At the entrance stands St. Michael's statue, dating from the early 17th century, and the Baroque confessional is of the same period. The adjacent chapel is that of **St. Sigismund (Kaple sv. Zigmunda)**, which marks the extent of Charles IV's original Gothic Cathedral in the 14th century.

Presbytery (Kněžiště)
Light falls onto the central choir through stained windows (1946-48) by Max Švabinský. The high altar was created from argillite by J. Kranner in 1868-71, and the Archbishop's throne and canons' benches are of the 17th century. The Late Renaissance pulpit is of gilded linden wood. Below the windows of the Choir is the gallery of busts already mentioned.

Choir, north end of transverse nave, St. Vitus' Cathedral

The Royal Tomb (Královské mauzoleum) is located in front of the Presbytery. Created in 1566-89 it is the work of the Netherlandish sculptor A. Collin. On its upper panel are figures of Ferdinand I with his consort Anne of Jagiello and their son Maximilian II; their remains have been concealed here for over four hundred years. A Renaissance balustrade from the latter half of the 16th century surrounds the tomb. In the northern part of the transverse nave there is a **Renaissance choir (Kruchta)** built in 1557-61. The organ is contained here on first-floor level, and the original Baroque organ loft is to be seen above it. The side arcades **The Choir Chapel (Kaple kůrová)** contain doors (decorated with relief work) which stood in the original facade in 1639. From The **New Sacristy (Nová sakristie)** a staircase leads to the **Treasury (Klenotnice)** in which are housed sacred objects dating from the 6th to the 19th century. Among the treasures here are St. Vitus' coat of mail, helmet and sword. Continuing around the Cathedral, we meet with the **New Archbishops' Chapel (Kaple arcibiskupská), the Schwarzenberg Chapel (Kaple Schwarzenberská)**, with its beautiful 16th century triptych; and the **Chapel of the Bartoň Family of Dobenín (Kaple Bartoňů z Dobenína)**, dominated by a Gothic altar c. 1400 and now dedicated to St. Anne of Bohemia.

Hilbert' s Staircase

The Third Courtyard

And so we have taken a look at St. Vitus'. Should you have left the Cathedral by the same door through which you entered it, then you now have a last chance to send your friends at home a postcard from Prague Castle, because the building directly facing you houses the Post Office. Here you can pause for thought and a short rest on one of the stone seats outside the building of the Castle Police and write home to your loved ones. But first read (for inspiration's sake) this extract from a letter once written by a certain nobleman...

Bohuslav Hasištejn-
Prague's Aspect and the Ways of its Inhabitants

I wanted to write to you something about Prague, that city more vast and glorious than all others, and of the ways of those who live there.

Old and Lesser Prague are connected by a stone bridge with an orna- mented tower at each of its ends. The Lesser Town was at one time, an unattractive sight, being quite in ruins. Its poor and needy inhabi- tants led the basest lives. Nowadays, however, under King Vladislav there is no doubt that the townsfolk shall soon be on their way toward neatness and prosperity, so long as the old disputes do not arise again. And that is how things look in Prague.

As for the city's inhabitants, they attend well to their stomachs and, considering nothing else on earth to be as desirable as food and drink, look upon moderation in this sphere as a true sin.They should be ashamed of their drunkenness, for they drink publicly in the streets, one man with tankard in hand soon being joined by others. They while away the time in beer-halls with debates and stories of various kinds, using their drinking houses as the Wallachians their bathing houses. They talk, presenting suppositions as actual fact and their own fictions as news gleaned from others.They behave affably towards strangers, detesting only the Germans.The women are gracefully formed, re- served, portly and full-bodied.Their speech is mellow, their eyes are charming. It is permissible to embrace them in the company of their husbands, although a kiss is regarded as a sign of impudence. Their complexions are inclined to voluptuousness, and a lack of self-restraint here can lead to addiction.

A tremendous impulsiveness predominates in the area of religion; a man may turn to any faith he should choose, and is not barred from it. Passing quickly over the Wycliffites and Picardyans I will say that there are men here who deny that Jesus Christ, is of God; men who claim that our spirit perishes along with our body when we meet with death; whilst others infer that it is well possible to find redemption through any faith whatsoever. Some even spread it about that Heaven and Hell are mere fabrication. There are also countless others about whom I shall intentionally refrain from writing. And all of this is not simply contem- plated in private but borne openly and in public. Every sect which emerges finds men who are happy to follow it. Such is their constant craving for novelty!

They are stout-hearted folk and proud, as if no neighbouring state had ever proved itself their equal in bravery! Their tempers flare up easily and, once they are fighting, it is not easy to pacify them. They fly at whatever their passion and fury are able to find fault with, paying no heed to warnings. First under Wenceslas and than again under Sigis-

The Third Courtyard

St. Vitus' Cathedral (southern facade), Main Tower

mund they took the town hall by storm, striking with their swords all those within, or else throwing them out through the windows. Nature has endowed these people with wit, however their profligacy and sloth-fulness renders their characters dull, so that it is impossible to find one decent craftsmen among thousands of men. Their lawyers, however, possess a good measure of sound eloquence."

The Old Provost's Residence (Staré proboštství)

Now that you've posted your greetings-original and witty ones, of course- let us move on to take a look at the Third Courtyard. As you turn left around the Cathedral, take note of the building which joins it at this point; it is the former Presbytery, originally the Romanesque Bishop's Palace, founded probably during the 10th century. Around 1660 it was rebuilt in the Baroque style, and its portal and corner stat-ue of St. Wenceslas date from that time. A Romanesque window is preserved in the east wall.

The Statue of St. George (sv. Jiří)

At last we have a full view of the largest Courtyard, and standing before the Cathedral we can see on its granite pedestal the equestrian statue of St. George, proof of the fact that the brothers George and Martin of Cluj, who created the work in 1373, really were masters of the art of metal-founding. The statue was damaged in a fire in 1541 and again during the period of Maximilian II's coronation in 1562, mak-ing repairs necessary.

The Monolith
Nearby the granite **Monolith** towers 18 metres high. It was erected in 1928 to mark an important anniversary; the Republic of that time had reached ten years of age.
From this spacious Courtyard you can take a step back and admire the imposing southern facade of St. Vitus. To the left, next to the Old Presbytery, is a low canopy below which lie the foundations of the Romanesque Bishop's Chapel and remains of the Spytihněv Basilica.

The Great Spire
In the centre of the southern facade is the Great Spire, which stands almost 100 metres high and was begun by Petr Parléř in1396. Following wars and other periods of unrest, the Gothic tower built by Parléř was eventually given its Renaissance gallery by B. Wohlmuth , H. Tirol in 1562, Pacassi adding the onion-shaped roof in 1770. The tower clock dates from the period of Rudolf II and has two dials, the upper (4.25 m in diameter) giving the hours and the lower (diameter 3.83 m) the quarter-hours. The first floor of the tower contains "Sigismund", the largest bell in Bohemia, as mentioned above, and dating from 1549. The second floor houses three additional bells: "Wenceslas" (cast in 1542), "John the Baptist" (1546) and "Joseph" (1602).

The Golden Portal (Zlatá Brána)
Alongside the tower of the Great Spire is the imposing triple-arched Golden Portal, the ceremonial entrance to the Cathedral. The grilles here are modern, whilst the Gothic mosaic above the Portal was initiated by Charles IV. Realized after Greek models, it depicts the Last Judgement. The central panel shows the Czech patron saints with Charles and his consort (Eliška Pomořanská) kneeling below them.

St. Vitus' Cathedral, Golden Portal

The Southern Wing
The Courtyard is enclosed on two sides by three-story buildings which date from 1755- 61 (reign of Maria Theresa). Pacassi's classicized facades here mask the fact that these buildings are actually older. The long facade directly facing the Cathedral conceals a mixture of Gothic, Renaissance and Early Baroque structures.

This site was once lived on. The old Rudolf Palace (1579) reached as far as this spot, and the house which Ferdinand III built in 1640 for his wife the Empress Marie Anna of Spain also stood here. In the left-hand corner of the courtyard is a low portal bearing the epigraph "F III". Just to the west of the Empress' Palace resided Maximilian II, and not far away stood the castle kitchens.

Entrance to the Gardens
At the end of this block to the left are steps leading to the Castle gardens-to the Paradise Garden and the Garden on the Ramparts.

The Old Royal Palace,
home of the Princes and Kings of the Czech lands (cross-section):

6   Vladislav Hall
8   The Observation Terrace
9   The Maria Theresa Wing
12 The Riders' Staircase
15 The New Land Rolls
16 Charles' Hall
17 The Přemysl arcades
18 Soběslav's Palace

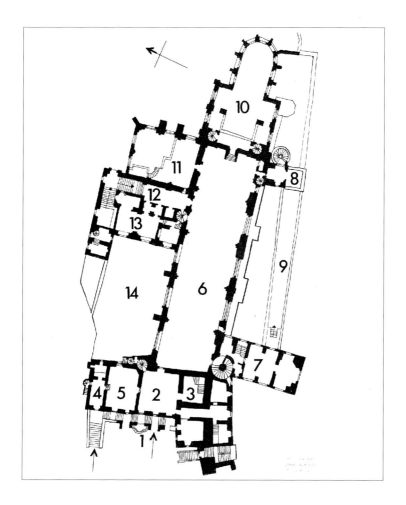

The Old Royal Palace, (ground-plan):

1 The Eagle Fountain
2 Antechamber
3 Romanesque Tower
4 The "Vladislav Bedchamber"
5 The Green Chamber
6 Vladislav Hall
7 The Czech Chancellery
8 The Observation Terrace
9 The Maria Theresa Wing
10 All Saints' Chapel
11 The Hall of the Diet
12 The Riders' Staircase
13 New apelace
14 North courtyard of the Old Palace

Vaulting of the Vladislav Bedchamber

Green Chamber , fresco depicting the Court of Solomon

The complex of buildings which lines the left-hand (eastern) side of the Courtyard is perhaps the most interesting here, certainly from a historical and archaeological point of view. It comprises **The Old Royal Palace (Starý královský palác)**
There surely cannot be many places in the world where such intensive building, extending and rebuilding has been carried out repeatedly over hundreds of years and on such a small area of land as here, in this part of the Castle. The land was ruled from this very place from the time of the Czech princes a thousand years ago until the Hapsburgs' decision to take up their new place residence at the opposite end of the hilltop, the Old Palace then being given over to offices, meetings and banquets.
Deep below the ground here fragments of the 12th- century palace of Soběslav and Vladislav are preserved. Later palaces were built above it by Charles IV and Wenceslas IV, and these are partially preserved at ground level.

The Vladislav Hall (Vladislavský sál)
When Vladislav de Jagiello again rebuilt and extended the Royal Palace at the end of the 15th century a ceremonial Throne Room appeared, at that time the largest of its kind inPrague. Still today the Vladislav Hall, as it is known, bears witness to the most significant of events, including the Presidential Elections of the Republic. If you stand at the entrance to the Old Royal Palace (and here note Pacassi's 1762 portico), then you will see from here the top of the Vladislav Hall reaching above the roof of the Palace.

Eagle Fountain (Orlí kašna)
At this same entrance do not let the 1664 Eagle Fountain (Orlí kašna) of Francesco de Torre, with its Tuscan column, escape your notice.

"Vladislav Bedchamber", interior detail

The Old Royal Palace
The first room you will see is the simple and quite empty Entrance Hall. The third story of the old Romanesque tower (from the middle of the 12th century) forms the right-hand wall of this Hall.

The Green Chamber (Zelená světnice)
The inlaid Renaissance door on the left leads into the Green Chamber, which dates from the 14th century. The chamber once possessed a Gothic vault which perished during the fire already mentioned above, today's ceiling being decorated with a fresco depicting the Court of Solomon. A part of the Renaissance ceramic tile work is original, as is the Baroque Dutch stove. Court sessions were held in this room from 1512 onwards.

Beyond the Green Chamber there are two smaller Gothic rooms, both modified in 1486 by H. Spiess of Frankfurt-am-Main and decorated with the emblems of the lands of the Czech Crown and members of the court. The two rooms are separated from one another by a low portal.

The Vladislav Hall
The Entrance Hall through which you passed leads also to the Vladislav Hall, whose vault you have already had a glimpse of from outside. This ceremonial hall is 62m long, 16m wide and13m high, and is probably the most beautiful Late Gothic piece in Central Europe. Benedict Ried of Piesting built the Hall in 1493 - 1502, during the reign of Vladislav of Jagiello. Charles IV had possessed three Gothic rooms on this same sight, although almost nothing of them remains. Tall windows (original Renaissance design) let light into the Hall from two sides, and you will notice the date 1493 above the final window on the left. Bold and stunning is the Hall's round-ribbed stellar vaulting, from which hang five Renaissance chandeliers.

Vladislav Hall

The Czech Chancellery

Hall of the Imperial Court Council

The Ludvík Palace
In the right-hand corner of the Vladislav Hall there is a doorway leading to the Renaissance Wing known as the Ludvík Palace and built in 1503-10 by Benedict Ried.

First you will step into the Chambers of the **The Czech Chancellery (Česká kancelář)**. The lower officials gathered in the first of these rooms, whilst the Chancellor himself sat in the second. In 1618 the Catholic governors William Slavata of Chlum and Jaroslav Bořita of Martinice, together with their secretary, were thrown from the windows of this second chamber by representatives of the Protestant Estates, an event which led to the uprising of the Estates and the beginning of the Thirty Years' War. The victims of the defenestration, incidentally, met with good luck; they fell out onto a rubbish heap.
A vaulted spiral staircase leads up to the **Hall of the Imperial Court Council (Síň císařské dvorní rady)**, so named because the Council which at one time assembled here managed the judicial affairs of the Roman Empire during the reign of Rudolf II. The inlaid doors here are 17th century, and the portraits of the Hapsburgs are copies.The day of 19th June 1621 saw the condemning to death, in this room, of twenty-seven Czech men who had risen up against Ferdinand II. They were executed two days later on the Old Town Square. Some steps lead from the Vladislav Hall up into the choir of the **All Saints' Chapel (Kaple všech svatých)** built by Petr Parléř in 1370-87 on the site of the old (Romanesque) Princes' Chapel. All Saints' Chapel was

The Hall of the Diet

destroyed by fire in 1541 and so underwent reconstruction during the latter half of the 16th century. Later it was connected to the neighbouring Institute of Gentlewomen, which we will speak of later.

The Old Hall of the Diet (Stará sněmovna)
The beautiful portal facing the Observation Terrace will take you from the Vladislav Hall to the Old Hall of the Diet, which was once a part of the Palace of Charles IV. It was then reconstructed and extended during the reign of Vladislav. Following the 1541 fire the Hall lay in ashes, its vault having collapsed completely. Only a shell of charred masonry remained. The Hall owes its present-day appearance to Wohlmut's work of 1559-63. A full four hundred years of Czech history (up to 1847) have been written in this Hall, which housed sessions of the Czech Estates as well as of the Provincial Court. To the left is the Renaissance tribune upon which the Provincial Court's supreme scribe and his assistants were seated, and between the windows stands the Royal Throne. The Archbishop sat on his throne at the King's right hand, and behind them both sat the prelates on their benches. The seats of the supreme land officials lined the walls, and representatives of the royal towns had standing room in the gallery on the right. On the walls hang portraits of the Hapsburg family.

The Chamber of the New Land Rolls (Sál nových zemských desk)
On the walls here are painted the emblems of the clerks of the Land Rolls.The annex, built in 1737, houses the room of the Crown Archives (Korunní archív). The Kingdom's most important documents were stored here between the years 1838 and 1884.

The Chamber of the New Land Rolls

The Riders' Staircase (Jezdecké schody)

The Vladislav Hall is connected to the so- called Rider's Staircase by which knights on their horses were able to enter the Hall directly from St. George's Square to pay homage to their ruler without having to lose any of their knightly dignity by clambering down from their ceremonially dressed horses. The Staircase has an intricate Gothic rounded rib vault and wide, slightly tilted steps to aid the comfortable passage of the horses. From here we can make our way down below the Vladislav Hall to take a look at the oldest parts of the building and see the enormously complex development of the Old Royal Palace laid out clearly before us.

Soběslav's Palace (Soběslavův palác)

On the lowest level below ground is the hall of the 12th-century Palace of Soběslav and Vladislav, and the small area behind the hall lies directly underneath the original Chapel of All Saints.This space housed the Czech Crown Jewels during the Second World War. It is not open to the public today. You may however, take a look at the Gothic Palace of Charles IV on the level above.

The Gothic Palace (Gotický palác)

Upon returning to Prague from France, the young Charles IV discovered that he had nowhere to live. The Royal Palace was devastated, and so Charles decided that he would build himself a new, modern residence. As space was rather limited he had the ruined Palace filled in and his own Palace built on top of it.

Soběslav's Palace

The riders' Staircase

The Hall of columns of Wenceslas IV

The Chamber of the Old Land Rolls
(Sál Starých Desek Zemských)
The Old Land Rolls (property ownership records) were kept here, in this room vaulted on two low pillars, from the reign of Přemysl Otakar II in the middle of the 13th century. Irreparable damage was incurred in 1541, when the Land Rolls were badly scorched in the fire which struck the Castle. The site functioned after that as a kitchen and as the place of abode of the Castle locksmiths, who, it is said, enjoyed a beer or two on the premises. The Land Rolls were removed up into the Chamber of the New Land Rolls, which you have already seen, for their future security.

The Hall of Columns (Sloupová síň)
The Hall of Columns of Wenceslas IV, with its remarkable vault, dates from around 1400.

Our tour of the Old Royal Palace, a complex and impressive structure hidden behind a deceptively modest facade, ends here. Now, where were we, a thousand years ago..? Ah yes, on the Third Courtyard...

George Square (Jiřské náměstí)
If you walk through the arched passageway which connects the Palace with the oratory of St. Vitus' Cathedral, then you will find yourself on George Square.

Charles' Palace

Renaissance window (inscribed 1493) in the Vladislav Hall (detail)

The Little Courtyard (Dvorek)
Just a few steps further, and you can look down upon the Palace Courtyard. Above its Gothic arcades you will see the Renaissance windows (1493) of the Vladislav Hall.

All Saints' Church (Kostel Všech svatých) and the Institute of Gentle-women (Ústav šlechtičen)
Connected to the Royal Palace is All Saints' Church, built in 1370-87 by Petr Parléř and, following the fire, reconstructed after the Renaissance style in 1579-80. The Church is connected to the neighbouring Institute of Gentlewomen. On the site of the latter there originally stood the Rožmberk family's Renaissance Palace, reconstructed by A. Lurago in 1755 to house Maria Theresa's benevolent organization for women of impoverished noble families. The building had been royal property since 1600.
The imposing entrance is decorated with columns and sculptures created in 1755 by J. Klein.

The Basilica [Church] of St. George (Basilika [Kostel] sv. Jiří)
The saint to whom this church is dedicated also gives his name to the Square. The original church of St. George was founded by Prince Vratislav in the early part of the 10th century, and in 973 a Benedictine Convent was founded alongside it by Boleslav II and his sister Princess Milada, the church itself then being converted into a Basilica. The Convent was built to dimensions unusually large for its time, for that same year (973) saw the occasion of the founding of the Prague

View eastwards from the south tower of St. Vitus

The Basilica of St. George

Bishopric. It continued to function until 1782, when it was converted into an artillery barracks. The triple-naved Basilica (Church) of St. George is the best-preserved example of Romanesque architecture in Prague. Following a fire in 1142 it was restored to its (more or less) present-day appearance. The facade, however, is of the Early Baroque. The Chapel of St. John of Nepomuk (Kaple Sv. Jana Nepomuckého) was added later alongside the facade.The most beautiful view of the Basilica and Convent is probably that from George Street (Jiřská ulice). The columned portal here dates from around 1500, and the Gothic relief depicts St. George battling with a dragon.

The Late Romanesque **Chapel of St. Ludmila (Kaple sv. Ludmily)** was built onto the tower early in the 13th century. In the middle of the 14th century, when both Convent and Basilica underwent reconstruction, the Chapel was augmented with an additional floor in Gothic style. And now a look at the inside of the Basilica...

The Tombs of the Princes
In the centre of the Church you will see the tombs of the earliest Přemyslid Princes. Among them, enclosed within a Baroque grille, is the tomb of Boleslav II, the founder of the Convent, and on the right is the painted tomb of Vratislav, founder of the original Church of St. George.

The Choir (Chór)
The Choir, connected to the main nave by a two-winged staircase, is

Chapel of St. Ludmila in the Basilica of St. George

square with a semicircular apse, and on its vaulted ceiling are the remains of paintings from the early 13th century.

The Crypt (Krypta)
Below the staircase is the12th century Crypt, its vault supported by well-preserved Romanesque columns.

The Chapel of Saint Ludmila (Kaple sv. Ludmily)
The Chapel of St. Ludmila, mentioned above, adjoins the Choir here on the right. The argillite tomb of this saint dates from the 14th century, and the altar before it is from 1858. The Chapel vault was constructed after the 1541 fire, and its paintings are of the late 16th century.

Let us return now to St. George's Square (Jiřské náměstí).

The New Provost's Residence (Nové proboštství)
To our right stands the New Provost's Residence. Passing by this Neo-Gothic building, you will find yourself walking down a narrow lane which takes you around the side of St. Vitus' Cathedral and back onto the Third Courtyard.

Vikářská Street
This famous little lane bears the name Vikářská Street. Its first house immediately alongside the New Provost's Residence is the Deanery,

Crypt, Basilica of St. George

Renaissance Portal, Basilica of St. George (southern facade)

The Powder Tower

Provost' s Houses

with its Baroque facade built in 1706 after designs by Santini. The St. Vitus Chapter School also once stood here.

The Powder Tower (Prašná věž)
This tower, which was part of the castle fortification, bears the name "Mihulka" and entrance to it is gained by way of house number 38. During the 16th century the tower housed a munitions laboratory, and later the Cathedral's vergers lived here.

Vikárka
What makes this street really popular, however, is the ancient Vikárka restaurant. Even the President himself comes here occasionally with friends.

George Street (Jiřská ulice)
Turn back to George Square and continue along George Street. Next to the Institute of Gentlewomen (Rožmberk Palace) stands the Lobkovitz Palace, originally Renaissance (built at the beginning of the 16th century) but later reconstructed in the Baroque style by C. Lurago. If you continue just a few steps round to the left you will find yourself in Golden Lane.

Golden Lane (Zlatá ulička)
This little street lies above the Stag Moat, and along its length tiny houses, their facades painted in cheerful colours, lean into the Castle wall. In the 16th century these houses were occupied by the Castle's marksmen, various craftsmen and-as legend has it-by Rudolf II's gold-beaters, from whose trade the street acquired its name. Earlier this century Franz Kafka himself lived in one of them. The passage-way in the Castle wall just above the houses originally connected the fortification's towers, one of which is often said to be haunted...

THE CASTLE'S GHOSTS

The Daliborka Tower was once, like others of the Castle's towers, a prison. It was in fact named after its first prisoner, **Knight Dalibor of Kozojedy**, who was kept there during the reign of King **Vladislav II.** Tour guides, in an attempt to excite visitors to the Castle, used to

Golden Lane

claim that Dalibor was imprisoned on account of his revolutionary ideas, although the truth actually lies elsewhere.

Conditions in this prison were harsh, the prisoners themselves having to pay for their nourishment. The poor Knight Dalibor had to earn money for his food by playing the violin, and the few glissandi he could muster did not have them throwing roast chicken into his basket. He died starving, and that's not a pleasant way to die. The executioner ended Dalibor's life in1498 and since that time, whenever Dalibor's plaintive melody rings out-always at midnight and usually before a storm-the Fiery Countess can be seen hurrying from the Černínský Palace, which you passed on your way to Hradčany Square.

The Fiery Countess

This lustful lady was frequently at a loss as to what new surprise she could spring upon the male dancers of the Palace. When, with the passing years, her charms began to fade, she decided to try to attract her gallant knights' attention to her legs - for the legs, as it is known, age last. So she had a pair of shoes made from bread. During this period of disputes over food shortages! How they would all stare!

The first to pay her a visit was a rather intriguing knight, and scarcely had the court musicians struck up their mazurka and the knight taken his bow, when the Countess' new shoes burst into flames. The devil-knight sniggered contentedly to himself.

From time to time, just before a storm, the Countess can be seen dancing across the Castle's courtyards towards the Daliborka Tower in her flaming shoes...

The lovely Brigitta

A rather peculiar statue stands in Prague Castle's Basilica of St. George. Perhaps you have noticed it. It depicts a dead young girl with snakes and frogs lying over her body. This is what happened...

In the court of the Emperor Rudolf there was a young sculptor, Michael. Wandering in the area of the Castle after his work, Michael fell in love with the very young and very beautiful Brigitta. Their love was great, mutual. The marriage was approaching and Michael was looking forward keenly to their first night together, for Brigitta had remained inviolably chaste, allowing him no more than kisses. On the day before the marriage was to take place, Michael was required to travel into the neighbouring Kingdom. Oh dear! All that night Brigitta had to kneel before him and swear to him that she would remain faithful. And he to

her. And then they swore it all over again. His activities in that neighbouring kingdom were not, let us say, confined to the daylight hours, and when he returned home Michael, so much in love, was convinced that Brigitta too had broken her oath. Well, he strangled his supposed adulteress and threw her body into the Stag Moat.

Some time later they found her. Michael, having discovered meanwhile the truth about his lover, confessed his sin in tears and, before being handed over to the executioner, begged to be allowed to create a sculpture of his Brigitta as a warning to all jealous people.

And so it was. Now, always before a storm, the beautiful Brigitta slips out from behind the sculpture and embraces anyone she should meet, to take vengeance for that violent end with which her faithfulness was rewarded.

The Mauled Barber

This tale, is a short one. In his court Rudolf II had not only sculptors but also a fine menagerie, and in particular his beloved lions. Oh dear, did those lions eat! Their feeder well knew this and resented throwing them good meat, so that when early one morning he found Olda the Barber lying in drunken paralysis near the Castle distillery, following the night of his birthday celebrations, the lion-feeder did not hesitate... and the lions enjoyed a good meal. Olda, not waking from his drunken state, was eaten. Since that time he has haunted the Castle, his head still aching...

This trio of Castle ghosts is said to haunt the territory of the former village of Dalibor right up to daybreak. If a storm is approaching now you are advised to move on quickly and continue your tour of the Castle.

The Old Burgomaster's House (Staré purkrabství)

George Street starts to slope downhill, and beyond a wall to the left stands the Old Burgomaster's House, which was occupied originally by the Castellan, or castle warden, and later by the Chief Burgomaster himself: chief official in the city, and the king's deputy. The building was originally Romanesque, later reconstructed in the Gothic style. It attained its present-day appearance after the 1541 fire.The reconstruction work was carried out by G.Ventura in 1555-56. The Renaissance gables are of a later date.

The Black Tower (Černá věž)

George Street is closed by a gateway and the Black Tower, the latter originally a part of the Romanesque fortification (12th century). During the reign of Charles IV it was known as the Golden Tower (Zlatá věž), as its roof was covered with gilded metal plate. The roof of the Tower was lost in the fire. Stepping through this gateway takes you out of the Castle and affords you a final glimpse of Prague's "hundred towers", before you descend the **Castle Steps (Zámecké schody)** in the direction of the underground (station "Malostranská").

Further Reading:

J. Morávek: Pražský hrad (Prague Castle), published Prague 1929
includes translations into French and German

V. Formánek, J. Parkan, J. Svoboda and J. Zeman: Pražský hrad (Prague Castle),
published Prague 1965 includes translations into German, Russian and English

J. Burian and J. Svoboda: Pražský hrad (Prague Castle),
published Prague 1973 includes translations into German, Russian and English

Adolf Wenig:
Náš hrad, Staré pověsti Pražského hradu, památky minulých dob, dějinné příběhy
(Our Castle: old legends of Prague Castle, relics of earlier times, historical tales),
published Prague 1938

Jan Morávek and Zdeněk Wirth: Pražský hrad v renesanci a baroku
(Prague Castle: the Renaissance and the Baroque), published Prague 1947

The Old Burgomaster's House

The Black Tower

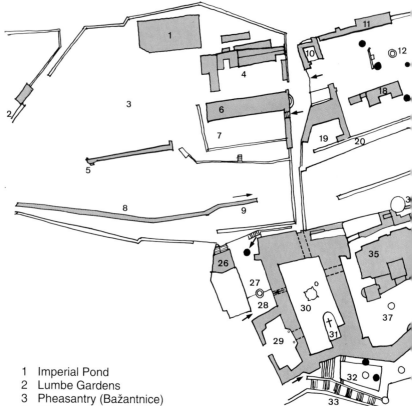

1 Imperial Pond
2 Lumbe Gardens
3 Pheasantry (Bažantnice)
4 Riding School Courtyard
5 View of the castle Vinegards
6 Riding School (Jízdárna)
7 Riding School Terrace
8 Upper Stag Moat
9 Brusnice Stream
10 Lion Court (Lví dvůr)
11 Glasshouses
12 Circular Fountain
13 Hercules Fountain
14 The Royal Garden (Královská zahrada)
15 Castle Guard
16 Singing Fountain
17 Royal Summer Palace "Belvedere"
18 President's Lodge
19 Stable Yard
20 Shooting Gallery (Střelnice)
21 Great Ball-Game Lodge (Míčovna)
22 Orangery
23 Fig-house
24 Lower Stag Moat

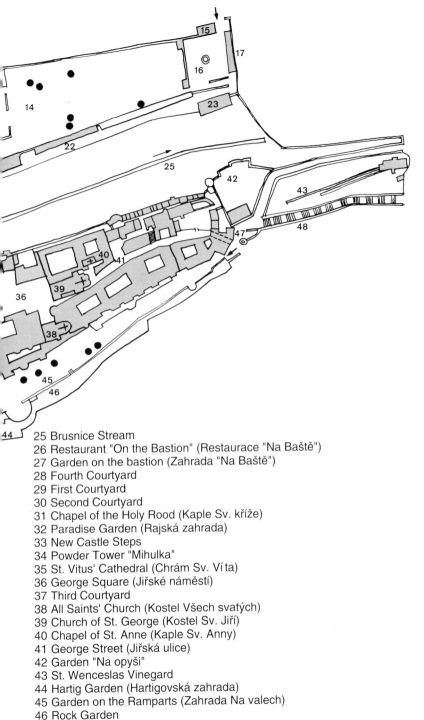

25 Brusnice Stream
26 Restaurant "On the Bastion" (Restaurace "Na Baště")
27 Garden on the bastion (Zahrada "Na Baště")
28 Fourth Courtyard
29 First Courtyard
30 Second Courtyard
31 Chapel of the Holy Rood (Kaple Sv. kříže)
32 Paradise Garden (Rajská zahrada)
33 New Castle Steps
34 Powder Tower "Mihulka"
35 St. Vitus' Cathedral (Chrám Sv. Víta)
36 George Square (Jiřské náměstí)
37 Third Courtyard
38 All Saints' Church (Kostel Všech svatých)
39 Church of St. George (Kostel Sv. Jiří)
40 Chapel of St. Anne (Kaple Sv. Anny)
41 George Street (Jiřská ulice)
42 Garden "Na opyši"
43 St. Wenceslas Vinegard
44 Hartig Garden (Hartigovská zahrada)
45 Garden on the Ramparts (Zahrada Na valech)
46 Rock Garden
47 Castle Vinegards
48 Old Castle Steps

The "Bellevue" Observation Pavilion designed by J. Plečnik

F. TIME TO RELAX

The Castle Gardens

Rebus poractis dulcissima quies.

*After work undertaken,
the sweetest thing is rest.*

Rest is always sweet. But particularly so in royal gardens. And you are fortunate in that you live in this century, during which the formerly neglected Royal Gardens of the Castle have been gradually reconstructed and opened to the public

We have already mentioned the architect J. Plečnik, who, won a competition with his plans for the renovation of the neglected southern gardens. Architects have continued to pay attention to these gardens right up to the present day.

Now these gardens are intended for your enjoyment; your tour of the Castle, although fascinating, has also certainly been tiring. So choose your garden, take a seat there and contemplate what you have just experienced. A map of the gardens is provided for you. Are you sitting comfortably? Then here's a little more Castle history for you.

The Gardens lie across the whole of the southern slope below the Castle; that is, the slope which overlooks Prague and is photographed a thousand times each day. The first of them is the Garden on the Ramparts (Zahrada Na valech). In the Middle Ages a wall and ramparts stood in this place. Various land restructurings were carried out here in the 1860s, during the period of Maria Theresa's extensive alterations to the Castle. The Gardens owe their present-day appear-

The Garden on the Ramparts with the former Rožmberk Palace to the right

The Ludwig Wing of the Old Royal Palace

ance to Josip Plečnik, who worked here in the 1920s, making use of the remains of the original Přemyslid ramparts, incorporating them sensitively into his modern design.

The Monolith
In the easternmost part of the Garden, on the Moravian Bastion, Plečnik built a Monolith with an Ionic capital and gilded sphere.

The Observation Pavilion "Bellevue"
(Vyhlídkový pavilonek Bellevue)
Some distance away, raised up on eight pillars, stands the Observation Terrace, which first appeared in 1924 below the building of the former Institute of Gentlewomen. In front of it stand I. Platzer's three "Torch Bearers" sculptures of 1770. Not far from the Pavilion there is a fountain with a Baroque statue of Hercules.

The Bull Steps (Býčí schodiště)
These steps connect the Garden on the Ramparts with the Third Courtyard. They are the work of Plečnik.

The Observation Terrace (Vyhlídková terasa)
There is a beautiful view of Prague from this ObservationTerrace which Plečnik built onto the original medieval bastion of the Castle.

View of Prague from the Bull Steps

The Hartig Garden (Hartigovská zahrada)

This garden, originally owned by Count Hartig, was not incorporated into the Castle's southern gardens complex until 1965. Early in the 18th century Hartig, being an avid lover of music as well as something of a composer, built here in the highest part of the garden his own oval, dome-roofed Music Pavilion (Hudební pavilion), and held concerts here. The ground floor of this delightful building has open arcades, whilst on the first floor there is a coloured stucco incorporating small mirrors. On the Summer Palace terrace there are sculptures by Antonín Braun, dating from about 1740 and having been transferred here from their original home in the Chateau in Štířín.

The Paradise Garden (Rajská zahrada)

The Paradise Garden dates back to 1562, when the governor Ferdinand of Tyrol ordered that the ramparts be filled in and a garden established there. In the centre of the Garden stands a Baroque fountain of 1703. The Garden once contained a great variety of architectural styles - the old aviary, for example, or the private baths of Rudolf II- but unfortunately nothing of these objects has survived.

The Hartig Garden

The Paradise Garden with Plečnik's granite bowl

The Matthias Pavilion (Matyášův pavilon)
The Matthias Pavilion, however, has survived. The Emperor Matthias had this cylindrical copper-roofed Pavilion built in 1617 in the southwest corner of the Garden. Inside, the Renaissance ceiling is decorated with the emblems of all the thirty-nine countries in Matthias' empire, and the wall-paintings are the work of J. Navrátil.

The Granite Bowl
Plečnik has gained wide recognition for his work on this Garden. The monumental flight of steps is his work, as is also this large bowl formed from a single piece of granite, weighing 40 tons and dating from 1924.

The Good Shepherd (Dobrý pastýř)
Near the Matthias Pavilion stands J. Kalvoda's statue of 1922, "The Good Shepherd".

The Garden on the Bastion (Zahrada na Baště)
The old bastion with its row of cannon once passed through this area in a north-easterly direction. Later the bastion was levelled out, although no garden was to appear here for a long time. It was not until the 1930s that an Italian-style "giardinetto" was established here. And by whom ? By Plečnik, of course.

The Stag Moat (Jelení příkop)
If you take leave of the Castle by way of the Powder Bridge (Prašný most), you will notice that a deep natural ravine lies on either side of you. This is the Stag Moat. As if Nature herself wanted to assist the Castle's powers of defence! The Moat was a very welcome component of the Castle's defence system. When cannons were invented, however, the Moat was no longer of much use, so that at the end of the 15th century Vladislav II of Jagiello built a huge wall onto its southern slope, and here the Castle began its transformation from mere fortification to grand royal residence. In the 16th century the Moat was given its name after the deer which then wandered in it. Even though the unfortunate animals were all captured and eaten by the French in 1742, during the wars over the Austrian inheritance, the name remains today. The stream which flows through the Stag Moat is the Brusnice.

The Riding School (Jízdárna)
If you continue from the Stag Moat along the Powder Bridge (Prašný most), then you will pass the Prague Castle Riding School on your left. It was built in 1694-95 after plans by Jean Baptiste Matthey. The part of the building projecting out in the direction of the Powder Bridge was once the observation lodge of the Summer Riding School (Letní jízdárna). The Riding School houses an art exhibition hall.

The Garden on the Bastion

Terrace garden of the Riding School

The Lumbe Gardens (Lumbeho zahrady)
These gardens lie to the north of the Riding School and are the newest part of the whole Castle precinct. They were not purchased until 1925. Here above the Stag Moat Plečnik built the semicircular Terrace which President Masaryk so liked to visit. Today these gardens are given over to the Castle's agricultural activities.

Lion Court (Lví dvůr)
Lion Court stands beyond the Riding School, at the entrance to the Royal Garden. Lions, the heraldic animal of the Czech Kings, were kept here in the times of Charles IV, and until 1740 the building housed also bears, tigers and various other wild animals. Today there is a restaurant here.

The Royal Garden (Královská zahrada)
This Garden extends from the Powder Bridge to the Royal Summer Palace (Královský letohrádek) or, as it is also known,"Belvedere". It was established in 1534 by Ferdinand Hapsburg above the moat, on the site of the castle vineyards. The work of Ferdinand and his son (Ferdinand Tyrol) was continued by Maximilian II and Rudolf II. An orangery and fig-house were built here, and rare bulbs and various subtropical plants were cultivated. Leisure facilities were built too, one of the most beautiful additions being the Grand Ball-Game Lodge (Míčovna) of 1567-69, the work of Boniface Wohlmut. The northern facade of the building comprises an arcade decorated with figurative and ornamental sgraffito work. (Whilst reconstruction work was being carried out after the Second World War certain "artists" managed to

The Royal Garden

Royal Garden with its Hercules Fountain

work a "goddess of the communist Five-Year Plan" into the original sgraffito design. What inventiveness.) Among the other buildings constructed here for leisure and entertainment are a Little Ball-Game Lodge, a maze, and of course the above mentioned Lion Court.

Night (Noc)
In front of the Grand Ball-Game Lodge stands Braun's statue 'Night', a remnant of the old Baroque. A sculpture of children playing with lions is also to be seen here.

The Royal Summer Palace (Královský letohrádek)
Another building here originally intended purely for leisure is the Royal Summer Palace. Paolo della Stella initiated the building of the Palace in 1538, and his work was continued after his death by Boniface Wohlmut (between 1556 and 1564). An arcaded gallery with relief decoration runs around the Summer Palace, which is regarded as the purest example of Italian Renaissance architecture north of the Alps. The relief work depicts scenes from history and mythology, as well as hunting and genre motifs.The building's original Renaissance roof structure (it resembles an upturned boat and is covered with copper plates) is unique and well-preserved.

The Grand Ball-Game Lodge

The Royal Summer Palace

View of Prague Castle from the arcade of the Royal Summer Palace

The Singing Fountain (Zpívající fontána)

Near the Summer Palace is the Singing Fountain, cast in 1564-68 by the court gunsmith and bell-founder Tomáš Jaroš after a design by F. Terzio. Stop here for a moment and listen to the drops of water, which really do seem to sing as they fall into the pool below...

Our tour of the Gardens of Prague Castle ends here at the Summer Palace. You will have seen some quite new views of the Castle and of Prague itself from the various terraces along your walk, and you will have realized that the views from these gardens really are quite beautiful, as beautiful as are the views from that slope at the edge of Hradčany Square where you began your tour of Prague Castle.

There are of course many unforgettable cities in the world, cities to

which the traveller simply must return. It is often said that if you throw a coin into a fountain or well, then your wish to return to a place will be fulfilled. But here in Prague we say that one look at Hradčany is enough - and your future return is a certainty. So go on, take a look..!

F. FINALLY... INFORMATION

*Ex parvis saepe magnarum
momenta rerum perident.*

*The outcome of great events
often depends on little things...*

Livy

One essential piece of information, is the telephone number of **Prague's police: 158**

Should you need to turn to your representative authority whilst here in Prague, just dial the appropriate number (below) to hear your beloved mother tongue:

Embassy/ Consulate	Telephone
United Kingdom Thunovská 1, Prague 1	24 51 04 39, 24 51 04 43
United States of America Tržiště 15, Prague 1	24 51 08 47
Canada Mickiewiczova 6, Prague 6	24 31 11 08
Denmark U 5. baterie 7, Prague 6	35 31 09
Finland Dřevná 2, Prague 2	24 91 35 94, 24 91 53 45
Greece Václavské náměstí 43, Prague 1	24 21 33 57
Hungary Badeniho 1, Prague 6	36 50 41
Japan Maltézské náměstí 6, Prague 1	24 31 11 08
Netherlands Maltézské náměstí 1, Prague 1	24 51 01 89
Norway Pařížská 28, Prague 1	24 81 00 01
Russian Republic Pod Kaštany 16, Prague 6	38 19 45
Sweden Úvoz 13, Prague 1	24 51 04 36

...so you can call your fellow countrymen and wish them "Good morning!" before setting off on your day's sightseeing. And where to..?

...to Prague Castle, of course. You'll find it with the help of our maps and tram number 22 (stop: Pohořelec) or metro line A (station Hradčanská and then just a short walk). We can even recommend walking to the Castle from the centre of Prague, along the route: Wenceslas Square (Václavské náměstí)-Old Town Square (Staroměstské náměstí)-Little Square (Malé náměstí)-Charles Street (Karlova ulice)-Charles' Bridge (Karlův most)-Lesser Town Square (Malostranské náměstí)-Neruda Street (Nerudova ulice)-Castle Approach (Ke Hradu)-Hradčany Square (Hradčanské nnáměstí).

There are, of course, other possible routes. Have a look at the maps and you will find your own-and that's always the best. Don't forget to gather impressions along your way-you'll write home about them later.

Postal Services
You'll need an 8,- crown (Kč) stamp to send a letter within Europe or outside it. Mailing of airmail items cost 9 crowns for up to 10g in weight, 11 crowns for up to 20g... and just as a warning, it will cost you 780 crowns to send a 2kg parcel!
Castle **Post Office** (on the Third Courtyard). Here you will find telephone and fax facilities. Letters sent from here are franked with the Prague Castle postmark.

Taxis
You will find these on Old Town Square, Lesser Town Square and Hradčany Square.

Toilets
Toilets can to be found in restaurants in the area, as well as   immediately alongside St. Vitus' Cathedral and the Nationalć   Gallery. Have some loose change at the ready!

Parking
This is available on Lesser Town Square between 8am and 8pm (or 10pm) at the rate of 20 crowns per hour. You will also find parking at Strahov. Vehicles may stand at Pohořelec for no longer than five min.

Guided Tours
at the Information Office (Informační Kancelář)
1.4. - 31.10.   9 a.m. - 5 p.m.
1.11 - 31. 3.   9 a.m. - 4 p.m.

40 crowns per person. Service not available on Mondays.

Entrance to the Castle
Tickets available at the Information Office

Refresments available at the Castle:
The "Terasa" Snack Bar, Expreso Bondl, Expreso u sv. Jiří (by St. George's Church), Café Erben & Erben.

... and finally as a memento of your visit, a few tasty and traditional Czech recipes to try out at home. bon appetit !

Hare prepared with onion

Ingredients: 2 kg hare, 1 litre dark ale, 2 dl red wine, 1/2 dl vinegar, 250 g fat, 100 g stale dark bread (grated), 400 g onion, 30 g salt, 1 g peppercorns, 1 g cloves, 1/2 a saffron.

Roughly chop the meat, add salt and fry briefly over a strong heat in 150 g of the fat. Remove meat from pan, add 200 g of the onion (rings) to the fat and fry just a little, not allowing the onion to turn yellow. Add the beer and wine, replace the meat and steam for about an hour. Add the breadcrumbs and spices and steam further, until the meat is tender. Place meat on a serving-dish. Strain the sauce through a sieve, add the rest of the (finely chopped and lightly fried) onion. bring to the boil and pour over meat. Serve with white bread.

Old Czech-style Chicken

Ingredients: 2$^{1/2}$ kg chicken, yolks of 10 hardboiled egges, 100 g white bread (chopped), 30 g fresh parsley, 10 g sage, 4 dl red wine, 30 g salt, 2 g ginger, 100 g butter (for preparation of meat), 50 g raisins, 50 g burnt peeled almonds, 50 g butter (for preparation of almonds and raisins), 150 g lemon.

Take the chicken pieces, add salt and fry until the meat is tender. Combine the yolks, lightly fried bread, chopped parsley and sage in a pan, add the wine. Srain the sauce through a sieve and add the chicken pieces in their stock. Bring to the boil and add the raisins and almonds (previously fried lighly in a littel butter). dress with lemon slices and serve.

Carp in dark Sauce

Ingredients: 1$^{1/2}$ kg carp, 500 g apples (sliced), 100 g bread (arbed), 200 g butter, 1 g ground black pepper, 1/2 g ground cloves, 1/2g saffron, 30 g salt, 1 g ground cinnamon, 50 g honey, 1/2 l red wine, 1 litre stock (or water).

Portion the fish, add salt and leave to stand for about half an hour. Fry the fish in butter in a large pan)or cook under grill) gradually adding the bread and then the apples. Blend the bread and apples and transfer them to a separate pan. Add the wine, stock (water) and spices and honey. Cook for 15 minutes, ten pour over the carp. Sprinkle with cinnamon and serve with potatoes or white bread.